Fleetcraft

THE ESSENTIAL OCCUPATIONAL DRIVER'S HANDBOOK

The Stationery Office

Authors: Jonathan Halliday and Philip Coyne
Design and illustration: Bill Mayblin

The Police Foundation

The Police Foundation is an independent research charity working to improve the effectiveness of policing and the relationship between the police and the communities they serve.

For further details of the Foundation's work and publications contact:

The Police Foundation
1 Glyn Street
London SE11 5RA

Tel: 020 7582 3744
Fax: 020 7587 0671

ISBN 0115522913

Printed in the United Kingdom for The Stationery Office
N172716 C20 10/04 19585 661755

Contents

Acknowledgements

Fleetcraft is a publication that incorporates a large amount of technical detail from the Police Driver's manual *Roadcraft*. The use of this material was kindly authorised by the author of *Roadcraft*, Philip Coyne, the designer, Bill Mayblin, Dr Robert West and the Police Foundation. Without such key support, this publication would not have been possible.

The author of *Fleetcraft* would like to thank George Smith of Minding Driving Ltd for freely providing expert advice in a number of areas.

Other essential guides to safe driving published by the Stationery Office include:

Motorcycle Roadcraft – The Police Rider's Handbook to Better Motorcycling
(0 11 341143 X)

Roadcraft Video – The Police Driver's Course on Advanced Driving
(0 11 341130 8)

The Highway Code – New Expanded Edition
(0 11 552449 5)

Driving Essential Skills
(0 11 552224 7)

Towing Roadcraft – The Essential Towing Handbook
(0 11 552022 8)

To order or find out more about these or any other driving titles, telephone The Stationery Office customer service on 0870 600 5522.

The guidance given in *Fleetcraft* in relation to signalling differs from that found within other editions of the *Roadcraft* series. These amendments have been made to suit the needs of the fleet driver, and do not reflect a change in police driving policy.

Managing Occupational Road Risk

Every employer who requires an employee to drive on company business is obliged to treat that activity in the same way as any other work place risk. This means that the Health and Safety Executive expects employers to have assessed the risks posed to their employees when driving.

The Health and Safety Executive have provided guidance on best practice in managing road risks this is contained in the document "Driving at Work - Managing work-related road safety". Below are some of the key recommendations of the HSE document:

Key Topics	Solution	
• Fatigue	Fleetcraft Chapter 1	✓
• Vehicle Safety Checks	Fleetcraft Appendix 3	✓
• Anti-lock Brakes	Fleetcraft Chapter 9	✓
• Seat Belts, Airbags and Safety Vehicles	Fleetcraft Appendix 1	✓
• Safe Loads and Distribution	Fleetcraft Chapter 2	✓
• What to do in the event of a Breakdown	Fleetcraft Chapter 4	✓
• Drugs and Alcohol	Fleetcraft Chapter 3	✓
• Overloading Vehicles	Fleetcraft Chapter 2	✓
• Journey and Route Planning	Fleetcraft Chapter 4	✓
• Biorhythmic Low Periods	Fleetcraft Chapter 4	✓
• Tachographs	Fleetcraft Chapter 16	✓
• Driving in Adverse Weather	Fleetcraft Chapter 4	✓

"Do you provide a handbook for drivers giving advice and information on road safety?"

HSE Driving at Work 2004

Fleetcraft ✓

About *Fleetcraft*

Fleetcraft is the first comprehensive driver training manual aimed at meeting the needs of the occupational driver. This book is based on the best principles for Advanced Driving as found within the pages of *Roadcraft*. Advanced police drivers use *Roadcraft* to train up to the very highest levels. *Fleetcraft* has taken these techniques and tailored them to meet the needs of the occupational driver. As a *Fleetcraft*-trained driver, you can rest assured that there is no better level of instruction. *Fleetcraft* covers many aspects of driving, including such subjects as attitude and behaviour, both of which are not only relevant to the company car driver but essential for road safety and an effective driver development programme.

The concept of Advanced Driving does not aim to encourage faster driving but rather safer and smoother vehicle control. By adopting the techniques found within these pages, you will find that you enjoy your driving more, reduce general running costs and, most importantly, arrive home safely.

This book is a guide that you will want to keep close to hand and refer to regularly. The principles found between its covers have been developed over many decades; if you are serious about becoming a better driver, then buying this book was the first crucial step in achieving your goal. If read in conjunction with the *Highway Code*, you have all the material you should ever need to perfect your driving, stay safe and on the right side of the law.

If you decide to read this book without the benefit of practical tuition, you will need to prioritise the way in which you tackle the content; it probably wouldn't be a good idea to start at page one and read straight through to the end. *Fleetcraft* contains many lessons, each of which may take some time to understand and perfect. Don't make sweeping changes to the way you drive, but take one element at a time and introduce it slowly to your driving style. Make sure that you have mastered each new technique before moving on to the next. Advanced Driving instructors always advise that effective observation is the primary key to driver development, so if you are not sure where to start, why not turn to Chapter 7?

There are a number of chapters in the book that can be read at any time and will yield immediate benefit. These are found at the beginning of the book.Take some time to read the chapters on dealing with driving conflict, driver fatigue, the mobile office and journey preparation, personal safety and adverse weather.

Any book on driving should be re-inforced with practice and high quality tuition. When considering practical driver training, ensure that you receive the highest level of instruction and confirm that your tutor teaches using only *Roadcraft* techniques. The system of vehicle control as taught here is the system that has earned worldwide regard and respect; royal escort and VIP chauffeurs around the globe have been trained using this system and put simply, 'it's the best'.

Many drivers are easily offended if their driving ability is called into question. We all need to learn how to deal with constructive criticism; an inability to handle this will reduce the effectiveness of any amount of driver training. However good a driver you think you are, improvement is always possible, and this is the challenge that should motivate you each and every time you get behind the wheel. The day you think that you have nothing left to learn is the day you should stop driving.

What *Fleetcraft* does not include

Fleetcraft assumes that you are thoroughly familiar with the contents of the current edition of the *Highway Code* and the *Know your Traffic Signs* booklet. Advice and instructions contained in these publications are not generally repeated in *Fleetcraft*.

1 Becoming a better driver

The mental characteristics of a good driver

This chapter is about how you can become a better driver. It focuses not on the physical but on the mental aspects of driving skills, and looks at how attitudes and concentration affect driving performance.

Research evidence shows that attitudes affect driving safety, but developing appropriate attitudes is not simple. It depends on recognising that attitudes are important, and on making a personal commitment to change attitudes that are unsafe. The first part of the chapter looks at the pattern of traffic collisions in Great Britain, and at what the research evidence tells us about who is at greatest risk of having a collision.

Understanding this evidence can be an important step in recognising and changing inappropriate attitudes.

Vehicle collisions

Most drivers think they are both safer and more skilful than the average driver – but we cannot all be right. In more than 90 per cent of vehicle collisions, human error is the cause; collisions do not just happen by chance, they are the consequence of unsafe driving practices. Driving safety cannot be thought of as an add-on extra; it has to be built into the way you drive.

Vehicle collisions

Traffic collisions account for:

- almost half of all accidental deaths in Britain
- nearly a quarter of all adult deaths under 30, whether accidental or not
- the largest single cause of death and injury for young adults.

Your likelihood of having a collision

Average drivers cover about 10,000 miles a year and have a one in seven chance of a collision during that time. Some types of driver are more at risk than others:

- those travelling more miles than average per year
- men
- younger drivers
- inexperienced drivers.

What are the likeliest sorts of collision?

We can also tell from the statistics which are the commonest types of collision:

- about a third of all collisions are rear end shunts – where one vehicle crashes into the back of another
- a quarter of all collisions are caused by one vehicle driving across another vehicle's priority
- around one sixth of all collisions involve a loss of directional control.

Do we learn from our mistakes?

Drivers at risk

Sadly, the evidence shows that we do not learn very well from our mistakes. Even after taking account of age, sex, annual mileage and driving experience, some drivers are consistently more at risk than others:

- if you have had a collision in one three-year period you are twice as likely to have another collision in the next three years
- if you have had a collision for which you could be held at least partly responsible, you are four times more likely to have a similar collision in the next year.

Repeating collisions

Drivers also tend to repeat the types of collision they have. If you have hit another vehicle from behind you are twice as likely as the average driver to do so again. If you have crashed into another vehicle after pulling out into its path in one three-year period, you are three times more likely than normal to have a similar collision in the next three years.

Driving too close

The practice of driving too close behind the vehicle in front gives a valuable insight into the way collisions happen. Because errors go unpunished – that is, they are not always followed by a collision – they develop into bad habits which increase the risk that one day the driver will be involved in a collision. Driving too close to the vehicle in front is probably the worst of these bad practices.

Driving too close to the vehicle in front is one of the commonest causes of vehicle collision. It is so common that most drivers see no risk in it. Half the rear end shunts occur when the vehicle in front brakes sharply and the one behind does not stop in time.

Resistance to learning from experience

These facts show that we are not very good at learning from experience. Most drivers involved in a collision do not accept that they contributed to it. If you think that you did not help to cause a collision, you will also think that you have nothing to learn from it, and your driving technique, together with any faults that contributed to the collision, will remain unchanged. To become a better driver, we have to recognise the resistance in ourselves to accepting responsibility, and take steps to overcome it. The first step is to recognise that we all have a resistance to learning. **Once we have learnt to do something routinely we are very reluctant to alter that routine, whatever the evidence that it does not work.**

Every near miss and collision needs to be seen as an opportunity to re-evaluate and improve your driving technique.

Have you experienced a near miss or collision?

Have you been involved in a near miss or collision in the last three years?

☐ yes   ☐ no

If the answer is yes, did the incident involve:

☐ a rear end shunt?
☐ one vehicle driving across another's priority?
☐ driver losing control of the vehicle?

Did the incident involve a driver (that might include you) in one of the higher than average risk categories:

☐ a driver covering more miles than average per year?
☐ a male driver?
☐ a younger driver?
☐ an inexperienced driver?

> What have you learnt from the experience?

An ability to be self-critical and learn from experience is one of the key attributes of a good driver. The next sections look at other positive and negative attitudes that influence driving skill.

What makes a good driver?

Good drivers have a quiet efficiency in their actions and this derives from:

- a good level of attention
- accurate observation
- matching the vehicle's speed and direction to the situation
- awareness of the risks inherent in particular road and traffic situations
- acting to keep identified risks to a minimum
- awareness of their own limitations and those of the vehicle and the roads
- skilful use of vehicle controls.

It is not simply the speed of your reactions that determines whether you are a safe driver but your ability to identify and respond to hazards. Being able to respond quickly to simple stimuli such as noise and light does not in itself reduce collision risks. Young, inexperienced drivers typically have very fast reactions to simple stimuli but have slow reactions to traffic hazards.

The ability to detect hazards is learnt like any other skill and depends partly on experience. More experienced drivers develop a sensitivity to the early indications of possible trouble. When risks arise they monitor them at a subconscious level in readiness to respond quickly if the situation develops dangerously. Because they are more aware of potential danger they are more alert while driving, and this helps to sustain their concentration. (*For more on concentration and attention see page 13.*)

How attitude affects good driving

How would you describe your attitude

to other road users?

to speed?

to risk taking?

Studies have shown that drivers' attitudes to other road users, speed and risk taking are a good guide to their likelihood of having a collision. Later in this section there is an opportunity for you to try two examples of attitude tests used in research studies.

Attitudes to other road users

Good driving depends on constructive attitudes and consideration for other road users. There is already a great deal of potential conflict on the roads without adding to it by selfish and aggressive behaviour. Such behaviour increases the stress levels of other drivers and increases the risk of collisions. Many drivers become unnecessarily angry when other road users interrupt their progress. You can reduce the risk of collisions for yourself and everyone else by being more tolerant and by avoiding actions which create unnecessary stress.

Attitudes to speed

The speed at which you drive is one of the most important factors in determining your risk of having a collision. The faster you go, the less chance you have of taking avoiding action, and the greater your risk of having a collision. Speed is largely a matter of choice – the occasions when it is absolutely necessary to drive fast are fairly limited. Good driving requires you to drive at a speed that is safe for the conditions.

Attitudes to risk taking

There is always some degree of risk associated with driving because it involves moving a large heavy object at relatively high speeds, but a driver's attitudes can greatly influence the risk involved. Attitudes which predispose you to risk are:

- enjoying the thrill of danger
- enjoying impressing passengers or other drivers
- disregarding personal safety
- the illusion of control, or overestimating your ability
- justifying risks because they are taken in a noble cause.

Young, inexperienced drivers run the greatest risk of collisions because they have a greater tendency to seek risk and disregard danger. They also see less risk in many traffic situations than more experienced drivers.

Many drivers take risks to impress other people – for example, young male drivers tend to drive faster when they have young male passengers than when alone or with female passengers.

Drivers tend to suffer from the illusion of control, which is a tendency to overestimate their ability to cope with the demands of traffic when they are driving. This undermines the accurate perception of risk.

Emotional mood and collision risk

Drivers commonly express how they feel in the way that they drive, and this can be very dangerous. Drivers who have recently had an argument behave more aggressively than normal and drive too fast and too close to the vehicle in front. American research shows that there is a greater risk of a vehicle collision during times of stress such as during divorce proceedings.

Traffic delays are a common source of stress and frustration. Many drivers release this anger by driving more aggressively and by taking more risks. If you are able to recognise this as a problem and can find other ways of coping with the stress you will improve your driving. Focusing on the present rather than on the purpose of the journey is one way of reducing the stress.

Attitudes and society

Our attitudes are shaped to a large degree by the society which we live in, the organisations we belong to and the company we keep. These groups help us to define what is normal, what is acceptable and what is desirable. We take on the attitudes of those with whom we identify. This is partly because it helps us to feel good about ourselves and partly because we look for approval from those whose views we care about. Large organisations can affect attitudes to road safety through educational and publicity material. They can adopt policies that reward safe driving and punish unsafe driving.

How do mood and stress affect your driving?

Can you pinpoint things that may have affected your mood while driving during the past week, for example:

☐ a source of long-term or serious stress in your life?

☐ an argument or other incident causing you short-term stress?

☐ daily sources of frustration in the journeys you make?

How often do you get angry with other drivers?

☐ never   ☐ rarely   ☐ sometimes   ☐ quite often   ☐ very often

How does anger affect your behaviour?

What in the past have you done to control your anger?

Because the attitudes of your colleagues and the organisation you work for affect your driving, you should be aware of what these attitudes are. Certain attitudes – for example, an overemphasis on reaching destinations on time, using language which is stereotyping or aggressive, or valuing speed and competitiveness – may undermine safe driving practices. Problems such as these really need to be dealt with at an organisational level, but the first step in remedying them is to acknowledge that they exist and that they have a personal relevance. You need to be aware of the social influences on attitudes and safety but, in the end, the responsibility for the safety of yourself and other road users is yours alone. Most people are reactive; if they encounter another driver with a courteous attitude and an obvious concern for safety, they are encouraged to adopt a similar approach. Drivers who have a professional attitude to driving and safety can influence the behaviour of other motorists for the better.

Changing unhelpful attitudes

Develop positive attitudes

We have now looked at driving attitudes that increase the risk of collisions. Positive attitudes that help reduce collision risk are:

• a tolerance and consideration for other road users
• a realistic appraisal of your own abilities
• a high degree of care for your own safety and that of your passengers and other road users.

You need to be able to recognise your own limitations and to be able to set aside personal goals in the interests of safety – an example would be restraining yourself from reacting aggressively to another road user's aggressive behaviour. You also need to make decisions carefully, taking full account of the traffic conditions and not acting unpredictably.

Recognise that attitudes affect safety

Understanding your own attitudes and changing them to reduce collision risk is a difficult task. The first stage is to be aware of the effect that your attitudes can have on your driving safety. One way of gaining some insight into this is the use of attitude tests. By answering a few simple questions you can gain some idea of your attitudes and a measure of your collision risk.

Research evidence shows that well-designed attitude tests give an accurate indication of an individual's likely collision rate. The questionnaire on the next page is an example of this type of test. The actual number of collisions for any given driver will depend on many things, but questionnaires of this kind reflect the way that people drive and accurately predict the risk of having a collision.

Check your own attitudes

Use the questionnaire on page 10 to assess your attitude to driving. Try and be as truthful as possible – the more truthful you are the more accurate the result will be.

If the table shows you to have a high collision risk, you need to think seriously about what you can do to change the attitudes that put you at risk. The next section analyses some of these attitudes and suggests how you might begin to tackle them.

Attitudes to driving

Listed below are some statements about driving. For each one show how far you agree or disagree with it by putting a circle around the appropriate number. For example circling 1 means that you strongly agree with the statement.

	Strongly agree	Agree	Neither agree nor disagree	Disagree	Strongly disagree
Decreasing the speed limit on motorways is a good idea	1	2	3	4	5
Even at night time on quiet roads it is important to keep within the speed limit	1	2	3	4	5
Drivers who cause collisions by reckless driving should be banned from driving for life	1	2	3	4	5
People should drive slower than the limit when it is raining	1	2	3	4	5
Cars should never overtake on the inside lane even if a slow driver is blocking the outside lane	1	2	3	4	5
Penalties for speeding should be more severe	1	2	3	4	5
In towns where there are a lot of pedestrians, the speed limit should be 20mph	1	2	3	4	5

When you have finished you can add up the numbers which you have circled. If you scored less than 15 you tend to agree with the statements. If you scored between 15 and 21 you are generally neutral on average. If you scored more than 21 you tend to disagree with the statements. Drivers who tend to disagree with these statements turn out to have approximately five times the collision risk of those who agree.

Acknowledge resistance to change

Most drivers would accept that developing a safety conscious attitude is important, but a problem exists because we believe our own attitudes are right and are reluctant to accept evidence that we need to change them. Attitude to speed is a key area where there is often resistance to change. To assess your own attitude to speed, complete the questionnaire that follows.

Driving speed

For each question put a circle around the number corresponding to the answer that applies to you during your normal everyday driving (not during emergency driving).

	Never or very infrequently	Quite infrequently	Infrequently	Frequently	Always
How often do you exceed the 70mph limit during a motorway journey?	1	2	3	4	5
How often do you exceed the speed limit in built up areas?	1	2	3	4	5
How often do you drive fast?	1	2	3	4	5

When you have finished, you can add up the numbers which you have circled. If you scored less than 7, you tend to speed infrequently. If you scored between 7 and 12 you tend a little to speed more frequently. If you scored more than 12 you tend to speed often. Drivers who indicate on this questionnaire that they speed often have about three times the collision risk of those who speed infrequently.

If you have scored more than 12 on the questionnaire do you agree that you have a greater risk of causing a collision, or do you think there are mitigating circumstances in your case?

If you do think there are mitigating circumstances, make a list of these and then decide whether they are genuinely mitigating or whether they spring from a reluctance to accept change.

Discussing this with a colleague could help to make your assessment more objective.

Many drivers who are fast, aggressive and inconsiderate are quite happy with the way they drive and do not accept that it is unsafe. They tend to think that their behaviour is more common than it really is, and that it is the result of external pressures rather than their own choice. These rationalisations create barriers to attitude change, and need to be challenged to allow scope for change. Recognise your own vulnerability

If you have inappropriate attitudes towards driving, and are able to acknowledge this, the next step is to identify safety as your primary concern. Consider the elements that bolster your unsafe driving attitudes and how you can change them. Most important amongst these are:

• a false sense of personal invulnerability
• an illusion of control.

These attitudes tend to prevent us from accepting that the risks of driving apply to us as well as to other people.

Critical self-awareness – the key to driving skill

Acknowledging the need to change attitudes is difficult because the evidence is statistical and most people trust their own experience rather than statistics. If you are a fast or aggressive driver, you may not make the connection between your attitudes and the way you drive even if you have been in a collision. Research has shown that drivers have a strong tendency to blame the road conditions or other drivers rather than themselves for the collisions that they cause. This helps to explain why there is a strong tendency for drivers to repeatedly make the same mistakes and become involved in the same kinds of collisions.

A fully professional approach to driving requires you to take an objective look at the facts, to be prepared, where there is evidence, to discard inappropriate attitudes and to develop a critical awareness of your own attitudes and capabilities.

These are key steps to achieving this critical self-awareness:

• acknowledge that attitudes affect driving performance
• be aware of your own attitudes and recognise that they affect your risk of having a collision
• recognise that you are vulnerable
• make safety your primary concern in all your driving decisions
• consider your own experience of near misses or collisions and what you can learn from them
• carry through changes in attitude to your driving performance by applying them in every driving situation.

Concentration and alertness

Concentration and alertness are also key mental aspects of driving skill. This section looks at the factors which can help or hinder them.

Our ability to handle information about the environment is limited. We cope with this by giving more attention to some parts of the environment than others and concentrate on them. This is important in driving because we react most quickly to things happening in the part of the environment on which we are concentrating.

One way of seeing this is to imagine your field of view as a picture – you can see the whole picture but you can only concentrate on one part of it at a time.

If you concentrate your vision on a small area you are less aware of the whole picture.

If you scan different areas of the environment in turn, you become more aware of the picture as a whole.

Scanning the environment

Drivers who can rapidly scan the whole environment looking for different kinds of hazards have a lower risk of collision than drivers who concentrate on one area. There are several ways you can develop your ability to do this:

• move your eyes around and look in all directions
• look for hazards in any shape or size and from any direction
• develop your sensitivity to the variety of possible hazards in different driving situations – this depends on learning, experience and a commitment to developing this awareness.

Looking but not seeing

What we see depends to a large extent on what we expect to see. You may have experienced, at one time or another, pulling out and narrowly missing a bicycle coming from the direction in which you have just looked. Errors of this type are common because drivers are generally looking for cars or lorries but not other road users such as bicycles or motorcycles, which they fail to see. When we concentrate we do not just look at a particular part of a scene, we look for particular types of objects in that scene. We find it easier to detect objects that we expect to see, and react more quickly to them. Conversely, we often fail to see objects that we do not expect to see.

In looking for cars and lorries, drivers can become blind to smaller, less expected road users.

Developing your hazard awareness

Some processing of information goes on at a subconscious level but a prompt can summon our attention to it. An example is the way we prick up our ears when we hear our name mentioned. Experienced drivers rapidly and automatically switch their attention to events happening outside their field of focus because they have a subconscious or instinctive understanding of the implications of particular traffic situations.

In the following chapters of *Fleetcraft* we analyse many examples of traffic situations for the hazards that occur in them. You may wonder whether so many examples are necessary, but their purpose is to increase your understanding of the potential hazards in each situation. The aim is to 'pre-sensitise' your awareness so that when you encounter a situation you already know what hazards to look for and can respond to them more quickly.

Instruction

Driver training at basic and advanced levels can accelerate your learning, enabling you to develop skills that you might otherwise never possess. Training can improve your hazard perception by making you aware of the potentially dangerous situations in different traffic environments, and by giving you practice in detecting them. But it is important for you to take an active role in developing your own learning. We each learn differently, and you alone can identify which methods work best for you. To learn effectively you need to have the right balance between instruction and practice. Instruction can draw your attention to parts of a task or ways of doing things but practice is the only way in which skills become automatic and readily available when you need them.

Overconfidence after training

In the period following training, drivers can get into serious difficulties because they overestimate their new abilities. On finishing a well-supervised course your driving ability and your confidence should be in balance. As you practise the methods you have learnt there is a possibility of a mismatch developing between your actual driving ability and the confidence you have in it. There is then a danger that your confidence will take you into situations which you cannot handle, and which might result in a collision. Recognise that this is a problem you will have to tackle whenever you learn new skills. Observe your own driving critically and drive within your known limits. Try to keep your confidence in your ability and your actual ability in balance.

The following chapters explain techniques of vehicle control that can help to increase your safety and reduce your risk of having a collision, but they can only do this if they are supported by positive attitudes, concentration and above all critical self-awareness.

Review

In this chapter we have looked at:

the risks of having a collision

the failure of drivers to learn from experience

the characteristics of a good driver

how your attitudes affect your driving

practical steps towards changing unsafe attitudes

2 The mobile office

It is highly dangerous to make or take a call on a handheld mobile phone whilst driving.

A great many fleet drivers find that their vehicles are far more than just tools to get from A to B; most view their vehicles as mobile offices. The vehicle must carry a wide range of communications and computer hardware, along with all the equipment and tools required to carry out a routine day's work.

Lately there have been huge advances in technology, and with this a whole host of new electronic communications and office equipment, much of which is portable, has been introduced to our daily lives. Before introducing any such equipment to our vehicles we must be sure that it will not have a detrimental effect on the general safety of our vehicle or its occupants. Any new piece of equipment that is introduced to a driver is likely to have a distracting influence, we cannot afford for this to be the case. Drivers, passengers and all other road users in the vicinity are all exposed to an increased risk of personal injury whilst the driver of a motor vehicle is distracted. A driver's main function is to carefully maintain full control of the vehicle being driven. In order that these obligations are met we must be alert, attentive and concerned primarily with safety at all times.

It is essential that we are aware of the dangers associated with attempting to use such items as mobile phones if driving. The golden rule is that drivers should never use a handheld mobile phone whilst driving; the best advice is to turn your mobile's answering service on. Even drivers who have hands-free systems fitted, need to remember calls should never be made when on the move, there is always a distracting effect when using any type of mobile phone whilst driving.

Some of us carry laptop computers, electronic organisers and even mobile fax machines in our vehicles. We must never attempt to operate these items or anything similar whilst driving. Always ensure that these types of devices are safely packed away in the rear of the car whilst you travel, so that you will avoid any temptation to look up information or use these items.

On occasions when you carry equipment, samples or tools in your vehicle, make sure they are kept housed in the boot or similar dedicated load storage areas within your vehicle. Do not leave items unrestrained in the passenger compartment as in an impact these objects may well be thrown forward at high speed. These projectiles, depending on weight, shape and size, may cause serious or even fatal injuries.

Now we can consider some practical ways in which the risks associated with unrestrained luggage may be reduced. The obvious solution is to place luggage items in the areas that are specially designed to carry them, and the primary storage area should always be the boot. If you have an estate vehicle or van, you should ensure that your vehicle is fitted with a load net or cage. If the items are particularly heavy then make sure they are tethered; most vehicles have suitable anchorage points fitted in the luggage areas to ensure that loads can be tied down safely. When packing the boot, always keep the weight as low down in the vehicle as you possibly can. The lower the weight the more stable the vehicle will remain when cornering, reducing any adverse handling affects on the vehicle and improving the stability of the load.

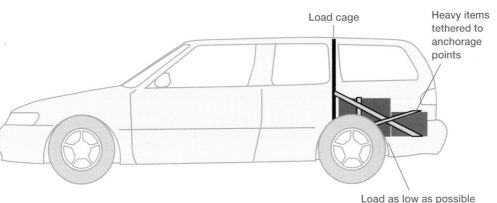

Load cage

Heavy items tethered to anchorage points

Load as low as possible with heavy items close to the axle

It is important to consider the overall weight of the vehicle when it is fully laden. All vehicles have a maximum gross weight and it is not only illegal to exceed the figure, but it can also be highly dangerous. If you are unsure as to what the maximum gross weight is for your particular car or van, you will find this information either in the owner's handbook or, alternatively, stamped onto the vehicle's VIN plate. The location of VIN plates varies from vehicle to vehicle and model to model. Common places to find a VIN plate are:

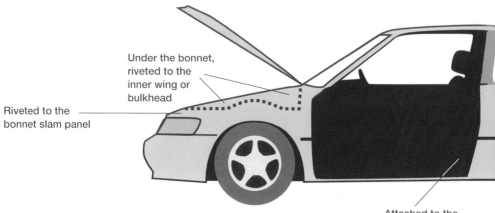

Under the bonnet, riveted to the inner wing or bulkhead

Riveted to the bonnet slam panel

Attached to the driver's or front passenger's door pillar

If you are unable to locate the VIN plate, contact your supplying dealer who will be able to point you in the right direction. Once you have identified the maximum permitted weight for your vehicle, you should visit you local public weighbridge where you can find out exactly what your vehicle and its load weighs; remember that the maximum gross weight includes the passengers. If you load your vehicle and you find that the rear of the car is significantly lower than the front and the steering is excessively light you are likely to be overloaded. Driving a vehicle in this condition is illegal and highly dangerous.

Once you have identified exactly what you can and cannot carry in your vehicle, you must consider the tyre pressures. Your owner's handbook will quote suitable tyre pressures for your vehicle when fully laden; ensure that your tyres are correctly inflated for the load you are carrying.

Navigational aids

There are a number of highly effective and efficient driving aids on the market at present, the most high-tech being the highly advanced satellite navigational systems that have the ability to pin point your vehicle to within just a few feet anywhere in the country. Using this system, you can enter your desired destination and the computer will guide you along your way giving directions where appropriate and ensuring that you take the optimal route to reach your destination. This system can be particularly valuable for the lone driver because much of the stress associated with having to drive and navigate through unfamiliar territory is removed. Many satellite navigation systems can be upgraded to allow instantaneous real-time tracking of the vehicle. This can be of enormous benefit should you breakdown, allowing the recovery agent to pinpoint your exact location. The system is also advantageous should your vehicle be stolen; it will allow the police to recover the vehicle quickly and without the need for high-speed pursuits.

There are other aids such as 'Trafficmaster' that will warn you of problems, such as traffic congestion or road accidents ahead, or other unforeseen circumstances that are likely to cause you a significant delay. With prior warning of trouble ahead you will be able to plan an alternative route avoiding the problem area.

If you are not fortunate enough to have any of these systems, there are many tips and tricks that you can adopt to make travelling in unfamiliar areas a little easier. The majority of vehicles produced today are equipped with RDS radios; these are a very basic but valuable way of keeping ahead of traffic conditions in the area you are travelling. When your radio is switched on, and tuned into the FM band, the traffic announcements feature will allow your radio to scan continuously for a signal that indicates a local radio station is about to broadcast a traffic bulletin. Once the signal is received, the radio will automatically tune into the traffic announcement and at the end of the bulletin, return to the station you were originally tuned into. If you are not making use of this system, it is worth taking a quick look through the manufacturer's in-car audio system manual to see if the system is available and learn how it is activated.

As a general rule when planning a journey, allow an extra 15 minutes for every hour you estimate the journey will take. The 15-minute rule is highly effective and it may be adjusted either way depending on the importance of your appointment. It is recommended that you never reduce it by more than five minutes. By following these few tips, you can reduce the likelihood of being involved in a road collision, road rage incident, or suffering from fatigue and stress. Remember that you should have already allowed for a minimum 20-minute break in every two hours of driving, and the 15-minute rule is always in addition to this.

A guide to route planning

You should never under-estimate the value of spending just a little time planning and preparing your route. You should never use or refer to a road map whilst driving. Many drivers find it advantageous to prepare a brief shopping style list with road numbers, motorway exits and other important reference points listed. An example of such a list is shown below.

Cardiff
↓
M4 East
↓
Leave J20
↓
M5 North
↓
Leave J11
↓
A40
↓
Cheltenham

This list provides in just a couple of phrases, the road numbers and motorway exits needed to travel from Cardiff to Cheltenham. A concise reference such as this will greatly simplify the job of navigating. By utilising such a list you are unlikely to miss motorway exits or take wrong roads. Should you compile a list such as the one above, find a suitable method to attach the list to the dashboard in a position that will not affect your view of the road, any warning lights, gauges, or controls. It is far better to have this form of quick reference available than to fumble with a road atlas.

3

Driver fatigue

Fatigue is a condition that affects even the best drivers. The key to ensuring your own safety and the safety of other road users is the ability to recognise the warning signs and avoid bringing certain physical factors together.

What is fatigue?

Fatigue is the result of physical and mental stress. It occurs when our bodies crave sleep or a change in environment. We all know how it feels to slip into bed after a particularly hard day, maybe after a day of intense physical labour or just immense mental activity. The effects of these two very different working days are the same – fatigue.

Fatigue can be induced through a variety of situations. Below you will find a number of circumstances that are particularly relevant to drivers. Drivers who are aware of these will find it easier to guard against this killer condition and recognise the early warning signals. This knowledge will provide a clear advantage in remaining safe behind the wheel.

Boredom is a common trigger for fatigue. The brain requires a certain level of stimulation in order to remain alert. If the level of stimulation falls too low then we start to become bored and boredom-related fatigue is induced. For a driver, this sort of fatigue may become apparent after driving for many miles along a quiet motorway or in conditions of poor visibility such as fog. Boredom is also a problem when we drive a familiar route over and over. There are a number of techniques that we can adopt to assist in reducing the monotony of a journey. These will be discussed later in the chapter.

Over stimulation will fuel fatigue. When the brain is subjected to a situation where high levels of concentration are required for prolonged periods, the brain can suffer from stimulation overload.

This sort of fatigue can be experienced if we are required to travel at high speed on a congested motorway. If we are driving in particularly stressful conditions we will find that our heart rate increases and tension rises leading to tiredness. This is a highly dangerous situation as it is in these circumstances that a minor error could have serious implications. Too many drivers fail to recognise the dangers of travelling too close to the vehicle in front. Introduce a fatigued driver to the equation and the knock on effect becomes only too apparent. The fatigued driver fails to react quickly enough to the car braking in front and a collision occurs. The resultant domino effect is plain to see, the driver travelling behind may not be fatigued but the slow reactions of the driver in front have reduced the following driver's braking zone. One after another, the cars following become innocent victims of the fatigued driver. This example shows the dangers of driving whilst fatigued and failing to leave sufficient distance between yourself and the car ahead.

Lack of quality rest can quickly lead to accelerated fatigue. An early start after a late night is a prime example of this type of fatigue. We are tired and unfit to drive the moment we get in to the vehicle. This sort of fatigue is usually found in a person who lacks in organisational skills and fails to recognise the dangers associated with driving a motor vehicle whilst being unfit through lack of sleep. If you have a driving job or are planning a journey can you really afford to be dancing the night away in preparation?

Environmental, drug and pollutant induced fatigue is far more common than you would ever believe. Our bodies are finely tuned instruments and as such are quickly affected by external factors whether they be environmental in nature or directly administered chemical preparations. There are a number of pollutants present in and around a motor vehicle that can have an intoxicating affect on the body resulting in drowsiness and fatigue.

Fatigue indicators – what to look for

Now that we have identified exactly what fatigue is, we can start to look at ways to guard against it. The effects of fatigue whilst at the wheel can be devastating, to drive whilst unfit is a serious matter, and over the years many a fatigued driver has paid the ultimate penalty for failing to realise this. How would you react to a person playing Russian roulette with your nearest and dearest? Remember as a fatigued driver you are that person.

Did you ever drive to a familiar destination and think 'I can't remember going through...'? most drivers will identify with this phenomenon; you may ask if it was fatigue or just a lack of concentration? The answer is both. The fact is that the route was familiar, and the brain was not given sufficient stimulation to ward off the effects of fatigue. Let's look at some more examples.

How many times have you seen a driver with their left hand on the wheel and right arm wedged against the side window holding their head up? Could this be a bored driver or a signal of fatigue?

Travelling along a quiet motorway early on a cold winter's morning you pass a car with the driver's window wound right down? What do you think? Hot flush! Or is the driver playing Russian roulette?

These signals are easy to spot. Along with these factors, drivers must constantly evaluate their own driving standards – any reduction in these levels must be considered a possible sign of fatigue. An indicator as to how fatigued we are is often measured by what external stimulation we are reliant upon to keep driving. If you have the windows wound down, the radio right up, then you know you probably should have stopped an hour ago!

Biorhythmic research shows that even if a driver is in peak performance, there are a number of periods during the day when we are more prone to fatigue than we may realise. These times are shown below in red.

am
12 1 2 3 4 5 6 7 8 9 10 11 12   pm 1 2 3 4 5 6 7 8 9 10 11 12

We may all be different but we all suffer from fatigue in the same way. We all know what it's like to try and fight off the body's craving for sleep, but like King Canute, we have no more power over the need for sleep than he did over the tide. Watch out for the warning signals and don't put off the inevitable, do the sensible thing and take action at the first opportunity.

Combating fatigue

Certain drivers may feel that the curtailment or delay of a journey is an unrealistic proposition. The reality is that once fatigue sets in, you cannot afford to keep driving. By recognising your limitations and adopting a number of simple safety practices, you will be able to reduce the number of times that you are inconvenienced by the onset of fatigue.

Use the following ideas to help you plan journeys and ensure you are fully prepared before getting behind the wheel.

Boredom

This is a very real problem for many drivers, there are a number of ways to combat its effects and maintain good levels of concentration. If you have completed an Advanced Driving course then you will probably be only too aware of the benefits of commentary. Every competent advanced driver will have mastered this useful skill. Although the road may be the same today as it was yesterday, there are likely to be numerous and varying hazards each time the route is travelled. The ability to commentate on each and everyone of the hazards will make for a far more interactive journey raising concentration levels and reducing the effects of boredom.

Over stimulation

When driving in a relatively stressful environment such as a congested motorway, it is best to reduce the number of stress inducing activities that we engage in. Avoid unnecessary lane changes, leave sufficient gap between yourself and the vehicle travelling in front. Remember that when travelling in these conditions, the only space you control is the space directly in front of your vehicle; ensure you maintain this safety bubble.

By adopting these principles, you can help reduce the rate at which fatigue will start to take effect.

Quality rest

Nothing can replace the benefits of a good night's rest before a day's driving. As a driver you must ensure that your working schedule includes sufficient time for a minimum eight-hour rest period between each new day's driving. Avoid driving at night when possible, if this is not practical due to the type of work you carry out, ensure that you take extra breaks from driving. Our bodies are naturally at their lowest between midnight and 8 a.m. Beware also of the low period during early to mid-afternoon, which is usually worse after eating a mid-day meal. Whether you are travelling during the day or night there is a place for boosting levels of alertness through short periods of sleep – a 15-minute sleep can provide a short term benefit, however, a good night's sleep should never be replaced with a series of shorter periods of sleep.

Environmental conditions, drugs and pollutants

We need to be aware that many over-the-counter drugs can have a serious effect on our state of alertness. One common belief is that winding a window down helps reduce drowsiness, however, this action may increase carbon monoxide levels within the vehicle causing further fatigue. The increased road and wind noise will slowly become an irritation of its own, fuelling our state of exhaustion. If you need to take any form of medication, prescribed or otherwise, ensure that you read the label carefully before driving. Studies have shown that we have a greater problem on our roads with drivers under the influence of drugs (prescribed or controlled) than with alcohol.

One common belief is that winding a window down helps reduce drowsiness, however, this action may increase carbon monoxide levels within the vehicle causing further fatigue.

Our driving environment is very important – a poor seating position, a dirty windscreen or a hot, stuffy cabin will all hasten the onset of fatigue. If your vehicle has air-conditioning make good use of it, by maintaining a constant temperature in the vehicle you will remain comfortable and less affected by excessive heat, reducing your susceptibility to drowsiness. If your vehicle is not fitted with air-conditioning then you should ensure that the car's ventilation system is turned on with cool air being blown into the vehicle. It may be beneficial to direct the air vents toward your face. Drivers who wear contact lenses should avoid directing air toward the face, as the drying effect will cause the lenses to become uncomfortable thereby accelerating the effects of fatigue.

Other factors

Food and drink

We are all aware that the human body requires constant attention if it is to operate at its peak both physically and mentally. An important aspect of this attention revolves around food and drink. A lack of food will have a negative effect in the same way that over eating will. When it comes to driving we need to ensure we are as fit as we can be – eating sensibly will contribute to our general well-being. It is important that the day is started with breakfast; an empty stomach will reduce blood sugar levels resulting in drowsiness. Eat light meals before and during a journey, heavy meals will drain energy as the body digests the food, leading to tiredness.

It is common for drivers to substitute sleep with caffeine. Caffeine does have its uses, but its limitations must be realised. As a drug, caffeine has both positive and negative effects; the positive aspect is that over a short period it can boost the body's levels of alertness and lessen the effects of fatigue. The dangers associated with caffeine are that once the effect has worn off, the fatigue experienced will be worse than prior to the caffeine boost. Caffeine de-hydrates the body, which again fuels fatigue. Never rely on this or any other form of drug to enhance your driving performance. It is valuable to drink plenty of water during the course of a journey because not only will it reduce the lethargy induced by de-hydration it will also ensure that frequent breaks are taken!

Exercise

It is beneficial to exercise on each occasion a break is taken from driving or after eating a meal. Some gentle exercises will help improve circulation, re-oxygenate the blood stream and generally improve the body's state of alertness. Similarly, gentle exercise following a meal will help ward off the lethargy induced whilst digestion takes place.

Eye sight

A driver who has only mildly defective eyesight will suffer from the effects of fatigue far faster than the driver with 20/20 vision. If you have glasses or contact lenses prescribed for driving ensure that you wear them at all times whilst driving. It is important that as a professional driver you have your eyesight checked regularly.

Remember that along with the obvious safety implications should you be caught driving with defective eyesight you could receive a large fine and your licence endorsed with penalty points.

The list below is a quick overview of the suggestions contained in this chapter on driver fatigue:

- ensure you have packed your luggage the night before travelling
- get a good night's sleep before your journey
- plan the journey carefully allowing for sufficient rest breaks
- share the driving if possible
- stop every two hours, don't drive more than 8–10 hours in any one day
- use the air-conditioning or ventilation system effectively
- monitor your driving standard, view any reduction as a signal of fatigue
- avoid driving through the bio-rhythmic low periods
- eat sensibly before and during a journey
- drink plenty of water to avoid de-hydration
- take time to find a comfortable driving position
- have your eyes checked regularly
- take plenty of exercise during breaks from driving.

Review

In this chapter we have looked at:

The main types of driver fatigue

How to deal with fatigue practically

The importance of regular eye tests

Being aware of diet and sleeping patterns

4 Journey preparation, personal safety and adverse weather

Many lone drivers suffer feelings of isolation and vulnerability when driving in unfamiliar surroundings. These feelings may stem from any one of a number of concerns. Some will be worried about mechanical breakdown, others are fearful of becoming a victim of crime, extreme weather or just the pressure of facing an unfamiliar situation alone. These are just a few examples of the worries that can haunt the lone driver. There are many ways that you can feel more secure whilst travelling alone. You will see some practical suggestions outlined below.

Careful preparation will make the journey easier and less stressful. It is sensible to give a copy of your intended route to someone who knows you are travelling, making sure they know the make, model and registration number of the car you will be driving. Supply them with an estimated time of arrival and details of where you will be staying; get into the habit of calling to say that you have arrived safely. These measures will ensure that if something does go wrong along the way, you will not have to wait any longer than necessary for assistance to arrive. There are many different types of route planning software available to run on your PC. These packages will quickly calculate the best routes available based on a range of your personal driving preferences.

JANE'S TRAVEL ITINERARY

London — Manchester
25th April

Setting off 8.30 am

travelling M1, M6, A56

E.T.A. 12.30 pm

Visiting Haydon Electronics
(phone 0161 345 6789)

Then staying Crest Hotel
(0161 987 6543)

Back 26th Midday

My Mobile no.
070 106 10832

Practical travelling advice

When travelling alone, it is advisable to pack a few more items than you might if travelling in company. If you do not own a mobile phone, it is well worth obtaining one even if only to make emergency calls. Just having a phone in your possession will considerably reduce the feeling of isolation whilst travelling alone.

You may feel more secure by wearing a baseball cap and padded jacket; the less vulnerable you appear, the less of a target you will be for the opportunist criminal.

Before travelling make sure that you have carried out the 'POWER' safety checks as outlined on page 178. Never underestimate the importance of having your vehicle serviced regularly at an approved service centre.

Make sure that your car is well equipped should you suffer a breakdown, collision or other emergency. A good torch, warning triangle, tow rope, first aid kit and fire extinguisher are all basic safety items that every driver would do well to carry.

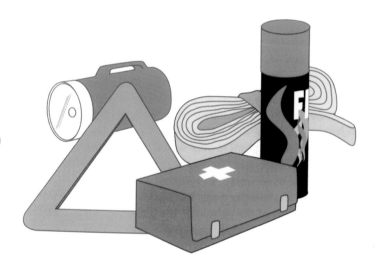

Consider the advantages of joining a national breakdown service; being a member of such an organisation will bring a range of benefits. Many drivers feel that the sense of security gained by being a member justifies the annual subscription fee in itself.

If you are unfortunate enough to suffer a mechanical breakdown, try and ensure that your vehicle does not obstruct the path of other road users. If you break down on the motorway, get your vehicle onto the hard shoulder before it finally comes to rest and pull over as close to the verge as possible. Although the hard shoulder is the safest place to be in the event of a breakdown, remember that you are still in an area of extreme danger. Turn on the hazard warning lights in order that other drivers can quickly identify that the vehicle is on the hard shoulder and stationary. Ask any passengers to leave the vehicle by using the nearside doors instruct them to stand well away from the vehicle preferably on the grass verge behind the protection barrier if there is one present.

Once you have vacated and secured the vehicle you should walk to the nearest emergency telephone. If you are unsure which way to start walking, look for the nearest white marker post – these are situated every 100 yards along the edge of the carriageway. They will indicate how far you are from the nearest phone and in which direction you should begin to walk. On a motorway, you will never be more than half a mile from the nearest emergency phone. Making sure that you are able to give the operator the number of the phone you are calling from, and the make, model, colour and registration number of your vehicle will ensure that the emergency services are able to respond quickly.

If you are a vulnerable traveller whenever possible you should call for assistance using a mobile phone rather than walk to an emergency phone. The advice for vacating the vehicle should still be followed, however, if you feel threatened or are approached by a stranger you should return to your vehicle. It is best to sit in the front passenger seat, lock the doors and wind down the window slightly in order to converse with anyone who approaches the vehicle. Once you feel the threat has past, you should return to a place of safety out of the vehicle on the grass verge.

Winter driving

A well maintained vehicle is unlikely to have any difficulties in coping with extremes of weather. During the winter, pay particular attention to your tyres; it is recommended that you have no less than 3mm of tread.

During the winter months, it is worth keeping some extra items in your vehicle should you unexpectedly encounter adverse weather conditions. Below is a list of items that you may find extremely useful should you be stranded with your vehicle:

• ice scraper and de-icer

• waterproof overcoat

• two pullovers

• pair of thermal gloves and an extra pair of socks

• silver thermal sheet

• small folding shovel

• sealed container of emergency rations such as chocolate bars, dried fruit and bottled water.

Although it is advisable to carry such emergency equipment, you should never start a journey if the weather is likely to become extreme due to heavy snow fall, dense fog or widespread flooding.

During the winter months, it is a good idea to ensure that the windscreen washer bottle is refilled a little more often than at other times of the year. Always use a proper screenwash additive, ensuring that you dilute it as directed on the label, as the additive will prevent the washer system from freezing. During the winter months, roads are salted frequently, which causes a residue to be thrown up by the vehicle ahead or vehicles travelling in the opposite direction. The resultant white film on the windscreen may need to be removed on several occasions during the course of a journey. The most effective way of doing this is by using the screen wash wipe system.

Driving on snow and ice

During the winter, there may be times when you may have no option other than to drive on roads covered with snow and ice. The first thing to do is to clear all the windows of ice and snow; not forgetting to clear the exterior mirrors as well.

As soon as you have started the engine, engage second gear, ensure that the wheels are directed straight ahead and let the clutch out gently. If the wheels begin to spin, reduce power immediately.

Remember not to leave the car idle once you have started the engine, start driving as soon as possible. Allowing the engine to idle will increase the time it takes for the car to reach its optimal operating temperature. This delay will result in wasted fuel and unnecessary wear and tear to the engine.

Turn the ventilation system on and direct warm air at the windscreen; this will help keep the windows clear of condensation. If the adverse conditions mean that visibility is reduced to any degree, remember to use your headlights.

Driving on fresh snow is much easier than driving on hard, compacted snow that is likely to have become icy. Fresh snow will provide a reasonable level of grip for good tyres; it is often easier to drive on fresh snow that is up to twice the depth of hard snow over a layer of ice.

The general principles for driving on these surfaces are the same. All controls must be operated as gently as possible, avoiding sudden or harsh braking and steering or excessive acceleration. If you find the car starts to skid, you must quickly remove the cause; this may involve releasing the brakes or reducing the amount of lock applied to the steering wheel. It may seem wrong to release the brakes or reduce steering effort, however, until the skid is brought under control this is the only solution. Once the car has stopped sliding, you can re-apply the brakes gently.

Remember that the key to driving safely in the snow and ice is through anticipation; you must anticipate the actions of other road users early. Braking on ice and snow can increase stopping distances by as much as ten times. Nothing can replace good anticipation whilst travelling in these conditions.

Many cars are fitted with anti-lock braking systems (ABS) and traction control as standard. Although they are invaluable safety features, it is wise to be aware of any limitations they may have. Traction Control will generally be of great benefit when negotiating ice or snow. A traction control system will match the power being transmitted to the driving wheels to the grip available; essentially this system will reduce wheel spin. An ABS system may increase braking distances in snowy conditions as the system senses the wheels locking, and releases the brakes more than may be desirable. The ABS system prevents a build up of snow in front of the wheel, which would normally be beneficial by increasing the friction acting against the vehicle, and reducing the time taken to bring the vehicle to a stop.

When faced by snow-covered gradients, it is important to try and keep the vehicle moving. Anticipate a suitable gear that will allow you to negotiate the hill while avoiding changing gears part way through the ascent/descent. It is generally more hazardous to travel down a snow-covered gradient than it is to ascend such a slope. Carefully assess the gradient and if you feel there is the slightest possibility that the vehicle may increase in speed and slide out of control on the descent, you should not attempt the manoeuvre. If you decide that the descent is safe, then engage a low gear; this will generally be a gear lower than you would use to ascend the same gradient. Make sure that you travel very slowly and are able to stop the vehicle at all times by gentle application of the brakes.

Remember that if you encounter these types of weather conditions whilst travelling, keep to the main routes and motorways wherever possible, these will be the last roads to close and the first to be re-opened. Winter road maintenance vehicles regularly travel the main routes during adverse weather; these vehicles generally clear any excess snow from the surface ahead and treat the road behind with salt. If you encounter a salt spreading vehicle, keep well back and never attempt to overtake.

If, prior to travel, you suspect that adverse weather may affect your journey, ask yourself if your journey is really necessary. Could it be considered a matter of life or death? Making the decision to drive could turn your journey into a real life or death situation! If in doubt, don't travel.

Should you become stranded ...

Should you become stranded in deep snow, it is advisable to stay with your vehicle. Do all that you can to keep warm. If you are able keep the engine running, ensure that the vehicle exhaust does not become blocked by snow. Keep one of the windows wound down slightly to allow fresh air to circulate inside the vehicle.

Avoid spending vital energy attempting to dig your vehicle out of deep snow – you will run the risk of suffering exhaustion and hypothermia. Avoid sleeping in these circumstances; sleep slows your body's metabolism down and, in this state, hypothermia can set in quickly. If a number of vehicles have become stranded in the same place, it is better to all sit in one vehicle rather than stay in separate vehicles. Obvious as it may seem, if you have access to a mobile phone, use it to summon assistance at the earliest opportunity.

Driving in wet weather

When driving in wet weather it is essential that you allow for increased stopping distances and reduced tyre grip. When driving in wet conditions consider the benefits of using the headlights to emphasise your position on the road allowing other road users to see you more easily. Regularly check your windscreen wipers work efficiently and the wiper blades are in good condition. Use the cars hot air de-misting facilities in order that the windows are kept clear of condensation.

One of the greatest dangers to consider when travelling in wet weather is that of aquaplaning. This condition occurs when there is a build up of surface water between the road surface and the tyre. This condition will reduce the effectiveness of both the steering and brakes. If you find that your vehicle has started to aquaplane, you should gently ease off the accelerator until the tyres regain grip.

Build up of surface water between the road surface and the tyre results in aquaplaning.

Whilst driving in wet conditions avoid driving through puddles on the carriageway whenever possible. The importance of checking your tyres and tyre pressures will pay dividends when travelling in wet conditions, reduced tyre pressure will cause aquaplaning to occur at lower than normal speeds. UK tyre law requires that tyres must have at least 1.6mm of tread, however, for reasons of safety 3mm should be viewed as a minimum particularly during the winter months.

Never enter floodwater unless you know its maximum depth. As a general rule it is only safe to drive through water that is no deeper than the centre point of your vehicle's wheels. If you do decide to drive through floodwater drive at a slow speed in first gear, keep the throttle constant and avoid changing gears. Driving slowly will reduce the amount of water forced up into the engine bay, thereby avoiding the likelihood of water interfering with the vehicle's electrics or entering the air intake. Once you have crossed the flooded area, remember to test your brakes, if you find that the brakes are not as effective as they normally are, drive slowly and apply light pressure to the brake pedal, this will create heat which will speed up the evaporation of moisture on the braking surfaces and linings.

As a general rule it is only safe to drive through water that is no deeper than the centre point of your vehicle's wheels.

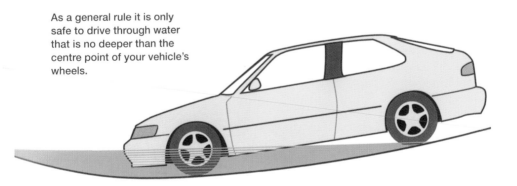

Avoiding criminal attention

Whilst travelling in an unfamiliar area it is unlikely that you will be aware of when you enter an area that suffers from an above average crime rate. Although these areas are generally few and far between, you can significantly reduce the likelihood of becoming a victim of crime by adopting a set of standard security procedures.

Keep valuables out of sight and resist the temptation to leave a handbag or brief case on the front passenger seat. Many a handbag snatch has occurred whilst a vehicle has come to a temporary halt. When carrying valuable luggage, ensure it is kept out of sight. If you use an estate car then it is well worth considering the purchase of a luggage area cover.

Many vehicles are now factory-fitted with alarm systems and immobilisers; make good use of these features each time you leave your vehicle unattended. Remember that even if you leave your vehicle for only a minute or two, it is essential that you lock the doors on each occasion. Criminals often target cars left unsecured on garage forecourts by drivers who have gone to pay for their fuel; some drivers have even left the keys in the ignition making things even easier for the opportunist thief. Make sure this doesn't happen to you.

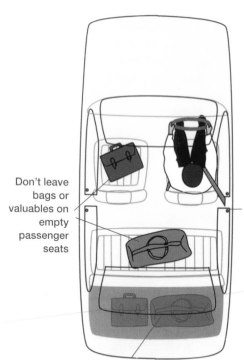

Don't leave bags or valuables on empty passenger seats

Make sure all passenger doors are locked

Always stow luggage out of sight in the boot or under a luggage area cover

If you need to park your vehicle on the road side overnight, avoid badly lit side streets, look for busy well lit locations where it will be more difficult for a criminal to operate undisturbed. Keeping to the busier areas will generally be preferable for reasons of personal safety as well as those related to general vehicle security. It is a good idea to invest in a good quality steering wheel lock, standard steering locks are virtually worthless as an anti-theft deterrent.

Many car audio systems are fitted with removable anti-theft panels. If this is the case with your system, make a habit of taking it with you when you leave your vehicle. Once a thief has decided to enter a particular vehicle, a search of the glove box and boot is usually the next task. The decision to enter a vehicle will often be based on what is on view. By removing the enticements, you will substantially lower the likelihood of a thief deciding to enter the vehicle in the first place.

Review

In this chapter we have looked at:

Preparing to travel alone

Preparing your vehicle for winter driving

Driving on snow and ice

Driving along flooded roads

Reducing criminal appeal

5 Dealing with driving conflict

'Road rage' is a phenomenon that appears to have exploded in the press, with incidents seemingly reported daily across the country. At the root of any violent driving incident is a person that suffers from some underlying psychological condition. A trigger for this irrational behaviour in many of these individuals is stress and a lack of ability to deal with its effects.

Driving can be a stressful activity. Drivers need to be aware of this and realise not only the effects on themselves, but also the stresses affecting those sharing the roads with them. Drivers who appreciate this will be able to do all they can to avoid becoming involved in this type of incident.

To enable us to understand a little better the two sides to this problem, let's look at the following scenario and see whether you can identify with either of the motorists. It is my guess that if you are honest, you can relate to both parties making it clear that on one day you could be the victim, the next day the offender.

Case study

It's 8:50 a.m. on a cold January day and Steve Millbank is driving to work: he's running a little late and knows that he has to present himself along with his monthly sales figures before the MD. The road has been fairly clear and progress is good. Steve knows the route well. As he contemplates his sales figures, he begins to feel a little nervous, anticipating and formulating his responses to the questions he may be asked.

It is only then he realises that he has caught up with a vehicle which is travelling a lot slower than he would like. He knows he will be late unless he can pass the car in front. Knowing the road ahead to be quite twisty with few opportunities to pass, he starts to plan for these 'golden' opportunities. As he gets ready for the first, he is frustrated by a queue of oncoming vehicles.

The car ahead of Steve is being driven by Sally Rogers, she is quite nervous as she is on her way to a job interview. It's not until 10 a.m. but she has already driven for two hours to get to Castleford, a town with which she is completely unfamiliar. She is also deep in thought mulling over many different questions she feels may come up in the interview.

Sally becomes aware of a vehicle travelling close behind. The driver of this vehicle seems to be trying to push her along. Sally starts to pay more attention to this vehicle. 'Back off you idiot', she thinks to herself. She speeds up a little to try and increase the gap.

Steve travelling behind thinks to himself, 'Oh no, as soon as we get to a straight, she's away, there's no chance to pass'. As the vehicles reach the end of the straight, Sally, unfamiliar with the road, naturally slows down. Steve can't believe it. 'What on earth is this car up to?' He increases speed and tries to push Sally on again. Sally is now getting very frustrated by the aggressive driving of the vehicle behind. She decides to slow down further in the hope that he'll pass and leave her alone. Steve is exasperated, he knows the road ahead has a series of bends over another two miles. He then makes one last attempt to make the car in front go a little quicker by getting even closer. Sally can't bear it any longer and turns the fog light on. Steve retaliates by flashing his headlamps ...

Does this sound familiar?
Have you ever felt like Steve?
Can you relate to Sally?

This little example shows just how easily other road users may misinterpret our actions and intentions. We need to be aware of other drivers' needs and to be sympathetic. Try viewing vehicles as people and not lumps of metal. Do you think this situation would have developed to this state if the individuals had been walking along a street? Why should the car make it any different?

From this perspective it is easy to see the two sides of the story. Humans have very poor senses which when fed ambiguous signals often lead to incorrect assumptions and actions, sometimes with devastating consequences. Once we are locked inside our vehicles we are left with just one sense intact – sight. Sight in many ways is the weakest of our senses. We have all heard the phrase 'the camera never lies', but how can we be sure that we have seen and interpreted the situation or information correctly?

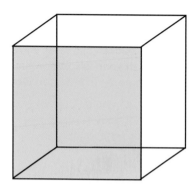

The brain's ability to interpret data in different ways is illustrated by this diagram. Is the blue face on the inside or the outside of the cube?

It is vital, when driving, that we are fully aware of the dangers associated with our inability to communicate effectively. This may at first seem difficult to achieve, but as we give it some thought, we will soon realise that we already have the skills – it's just a matter of rediscovering them and learning to use them again. Courtesy and patience are the keys to success. As the years have rolled by, motorists have become fully encapsulated within their vehicles, with air-conditioning, in-car entertainment and luxury upholstery now commonplace. Long gone are the days of wooden seats, cross-ply tyres, and draughts as cold as arctic winters. It was in these early days that courtesy was everything, time everlasting and people seemed to communicate better. Not so long ago, a wave of acknowledgement was commonplace. Now it's more likely to be interpreted as an offensive gesture and so often can be the start of a downward spiral leading to a situation that the media has dubbed 'Road Rage', others may see it more as the extreme effects of 'driving stress'.

Phases of conflict

There are three basic levels to this condition they are:

Passive

Active

Explosive

Passive. This is the lowest level and is identified by increased feelings of anger and frustration towards other road users. The feelings or thoughts may be contained or expressed audibly.

Active. This is where the passive feelings are acted upon and result in a driver altering the course of his or her vehicle in order to affect another road user, for example speeding up when being overtaken, cutting across the path of another vehicle or aggressive tailgating.

Explosive. This is the situation that drivers fear most, when our personal safety is seriously compromised. This could entail being forced off the road or being forced to stop knowing the other party is likely to carrying out a physical assault.

Each of these phases is progressive. It is unusual for a situation to start off at the explosive phase – these incidents generally build on a foundation of poor communication and misunderstandings. The ability to realise this and take action will help ensure that you never have to experience violence on the road.

In each and every occurrence, someone needs to take ownership of the situation. This doesn't mean accepting the blame but managing the incident to ensure that it comes to a swift and satisfactory conclusion. In order to take control, one must be aware of both parties' needs and concerns. Once these have been identified, it is possible to apply the techniques to attain the goal – diffusion.

We shall look at a wide range of solutions to various situations, some may seem simple, even common sense, but as we have already discussed, we are not re-inventing the wheel. We are simply applying the skills the majority of us have, but seem to leave on the pavement the moment we step into our cars.

When faced with passive incidents, it is the mental game that becomes all-important. If we are unable to control our emotions then the slope is a slippery one. Many drivers can say they have experienced some of the symptoms associated with the stress of driving. By learning to identify and deal with these situations, we can actively protect ourselves against being involved in such incidents.

The key is recognition. Once you recognise that you are becoming tense, angry and frustrated at other drivers, you must pause to consider the situation. Realise that the other car is not just a lump of steel, think of it more as a suit of fine clothes and sitting inside is a person who could quite easily be precious to you. Use your compassionate side to help you turn the vehicle into a real human being. If you are able to do this then you are over the worst.

 If you find yourself in a situation where the passive phase has been passed and the situation is becoming active, more assertive techniques may have to be employed. If we think back to our example involving Sally and Steve, we should be able to identify the initial passive stage of the incident and see how it rapidly became active. If one or both of the drivers had been able to recognise the warning signs, that incident need never have developed beyond the first phase.

Once into the active phase, it is imperative that action is taken swiftly as the explosive phase must be avoided at all costs. Once you feel that the other driver is displaying aggressive signs, it is in your interest to look for a way out. That may mean pulling in at a safe location to allow the harassed motorist behind an opportunity to pass. Remember once in the active stage you may be physically at risk. An impatient driver is likely to take risks and since these risks may involve you and your vehicle, you need to act quickly and effectively to ensure your own safety.

Once we enter the realms of the 'explosive' phase, you must realise the severity of the situation. Self-preservation techniques may need to be employed. If you have a mobile phone and are able to use it safely, alert the police to the situation using the 999 system. Be as precise as possible in giving your current location, direction of travel and any details relating to the offending vehicle. Listen to the advice given to you by the control room staff. If you are using a hands-free system, the police officer may ask you to keep the line open until the conclusion of the incident. Remember not to stop at the side of the road in these circumstances – stay on main roads and do not increase your speed.

If you are familiar with the location, drive to the nearest police station and when outside sound the horn to summon help. If you are unfamiliar with your surroundings and you need to stop, look for a garage forecourt, bank or building society. These types of premises have security recording systems and direct police alarms.

Try to gather as much information about the other vehicle as possible such as make, model, colour, registration number and description of occupants. All this information will help the police.

Remember that if you are able to identify the initial phases, you will be able to avoid ever having to deal with this type of incident. It is essential that as a driver you never seek to retaliate or set out to 'teach the other driver a lesson'. Responding in this way will instantly raise the severity of the incident to the active or even the explosive phase as already discussed.

Although the press may suggest that 'road rage' is a virulent epidemic, you must remember that in reality only a very small percentage of us will ever experience driving conflict at its most extreme. Practising the techniques outlined in this chapter will help ensure that you are never one of the few.

When we look at driving conflict, it is helpful to realise that the situation may escalate quickly. The conflict circle as shown below illustrates this. The cycle needs to be broken quickly and effectively if you are going to successfully deal with a building conflict incident. You cannot directly cause the other driver to break this cycle, you must remember to take control and using any of the methods discussed to break the cycle. The earlier the cycle is broken the quicker the incident will subside.

The conflict cycle

Other driver's behaviour

My attitude

Other driver's attitude

My behaviour

Below you will find a number of practical suggestions as to how you may be able to diffuse a potential conflict situation in the early stages.

- don't view the situation personally
- avoid eye contact with aggressive drivers
- avoid obscene gestures
- don't tailgate
- use the horn sparingly; the horn should only be used to warn others of your presence, not as a form of rebuke
- don't obstruct the outer lanes of the motorway or dual carriageway
- allow adequate time for your journey
- make sure you are comfortable in your car
- remember the conflict cycle
- be diplomatic in your driving
- be prepared to acknowledge your mistakes.

Review

In this chapter we have looked at:

How a road rage incident develops

The stages of road rage

The conflict cycle

Ways of avoiding confrontation

6 The system of vehicle control

The need for a system of vehicle control

The system of vehicle control aims to reduce the likelihood of a collision whilst a driver recognises and negotiates any hazard encountered. The system of vehicle control should be viewed as nothing more than a logical extension of the basic mirror, signal, manoeuvre routine that we all had to learn to pass our driving test.

Learning to use this system will help to give you calm control of your vehicle, and enable you to deal with hazards without getting flustered. Your progress will be steady and unobtrusive – the characteristics of a skilled driver.

Driving skills

Driving requires more than pure handling skills. Many hazards encountered can be unpredictable. The earlier a hazard is recognised, the more time a driver will have to develop a suitable driving plan and safely negotiate the danger.

Mental skills
The ability to scan the environment, recognise relevant dangers or hazards, decide on their priority and form an achievable driving plan.

Physical skills
The ability to translate intentions and thoughts into physical action accurately and smoothly.

In using these skills you need to take into account: real ability as opposed to your perceived ability (what you can actually do as opposed to what you think you can do – in the average driver there is a significant gap between real and perceived ability, and a key objective of driver training is to bring perceptions in line with reality); the capabilities of the vehicle; and the prevailing weather and road conditions.

Drivers have a great deal to think about and anticipate; road and traffic conditions continually change, requiring you to make frequent adjustments of course and speed. You need to take into account the activities of other road users and what they might do, the closeness of other vehicles, the need to signal intentions, the road and surface conditions, the weather, and how your vehicle is handling. The system of vehicle control simplifies these tasks. It provides a simple and consistent method of driving which ensures that you overlook no detail and leave nothing to chance.

> *The system of vehicle control gives you that essential aspect of safe driving – time to react.*

Hazards

A hazard is anything which is potentially dangerous. A hazard can be immediate and obvious, such as a car approaching you on the wrong side of the road, or it may be less obvious, but just as potentially dangerous, such as a blind bend which conceals a lorry reversing into your path. Much of the skill of *Fleetcraft* is in recognising hazards – the situations that are potentially dangerous – and then taking the appropriate action to cope with them. One of the main causes of collisions is the failure to recognise hazardous situations. If you fail to see the possible danger you cannot take actions to avoid it.

On the roads you will meet three main types of hazard:

- physical features such as junctions, roundabouts, bends or hill crests

- risks arising from the position or movement of other road users

- problems arising from variations in the road surface, weather conditions and visibility.

> How good are you at identifying situations that are potentially dangerous? Next time you drive along a route you use regularly – say your normal route to work – examine the route carefully for situations that are potentially dangerous and where in the past you have not used sufficient caution. Plan how you will negotiate each of these situations in future.

The system of vehicle control

The system of vehicle control is a way of approaching and negotiating hazards that is methodical, safe and leaves nothing to chance. It promotes careful observation, early anticipation and planning, and a systematic use of the controls to achieve maximum vehicle stability. It is a systematic way of dealing with an unpredictable environment. It is central to *Fleetcraft*, drawing together all other driving skills in a co-ordinated response to road and traffic conditions. It gives you the time to select the best position, speed and gear to negotiate the hazards safely and efficiently.

Driving hazards come singly and in clusters; they overlap and change all the time. The system accommodates this continual fluctuation by means of a centrally flexible element – you, the driver. As with the other skills in *Fleetcraft* you have responsibility for using the system actively and intelligently. When you use the system to approach and negotiate a hazard you consider and use a logical sequence of actions to take you past it safely and efficiently. If new hazards arise, you adapt by reassessing the situation and reapplying the system at an appropriate phase.

The five phases of the system

The system is divided into five phases:

Information	Position	Speed	Gear	Acceleration

Each phase of the system depends on the one before, and you normally consider them in sequence. Start the system by considering your information needs, and then work through each phase in turn. If road conditions change, consider the new information and re-enter the system at an appropriate phase. Use the system flexibly in response to actual road conditions; do not follow the sequence rigidly if it is inappropriate to the circumstances.

Why information is so important

Taking, using and giving information is the key to the system. It starts the system and continues throughout it. You constantly need information to plan your driving and you should provide information for the benefit of other road uses. Information allows you to adapt your driving to changes in road circumstances. It is the framework on which the other phases of the system – position, speed, gear, acceleration – depend.

Continuous assessment of information runs through every phase of the system.

Information phase: **T** take   **U** use   **G** give

Mirrors and signals

Constantly assess the situation ahead and to the side for changes in circumstances. Use your mirrors as often as is necessary to be fully aware of what is happening behind you.

At certain points in the system specific checks for information are important.

Before you change course or speed you need to know what is happening in front, to the sides and behind you; mirror checks at these points are essential.

Remember the *Highway Code* advice of mirrors – signal – manoeuvre.

Use of the horn

Sound your horn whenever you think another road user could hear and benefit from it. The purpose of the horn is to inform others that you are there. It gives you no right to proceed, and should never be used as a rebuke. It can be used at any stage of the system. Always be prepared to react to another road user's horn warning.

These pages set out the phases of the system

The information phase overlaps every other phase of the system.

Take information
Look all round you. Scan to the front and sides. Check your mirrors at the appropriate points in the system, and always before you change direction or speed.

Use information
Using the information you have gathered, plan how to deal with the identified hazards and make contingency plans for dealing with the unexpected. Decide on your next action using the system as a guide. If new hazards arise consider whether you need to re-run the system from an earlier phase.

Give information
Give signals to benefit other road users. Remember other road users include pedestrians and cyclists. Your options include indicators, brakelights, flashing your headlights, hazard warning lights, arm signals and sounding your horn. Generally the earlier the warning the greater the benefit.

Position

Position yourself so that you can negotiate the hazard safely and smoothly. Before you change position check your mirrors.

Take account of the road surface and other road users – including pedestrians and cyclists, especially children.

Speed

Adjust your speed to that appropriate for the hazard, taking into account visibility, the road surface, the degree of cornering required, the activities of other road users and the possibility of unseen hazards.

See Chapter 8,
Acceleration; Braking;
Gears
See Chapter 9, Avoiding skids

Use the accelerator, brake or, when on slippery surfaces, gears to give you the speed which will enable you to complete the manoeuvre. Make good use of acceleration sense.

Aim to make all adjustments in speed smoothly and steadily; early anticipation is essential for this.

Gear

Once you have the right speed for the hazard engage the correct gear for the speed. Choose a gear that is responsive at that speed.

If you have to brake to get the right speed, you can make the gear change before the end of braking. But always avoid late braking and snatched gear changes.

See Chapter 8 Except in slippery conditions, avoid using your gears as brakes.

Acceleration

Use the accelerator to maintain your speed and stability through the hazard. Depress the accelerator sufficiently to offset any loss of speed due to cornering effects.

Taking account of your speed, the road surface, the amount of turn required, other road users, and the road and traffic conditions ahead and behind, decide whether it is appropriate to accelerate away from the hazard.

See Chapter 8 Choose an appropriate point to accelerate safely and smoothly, adjusting the amount of acceleration to the circumstances.

Use the system flexibly

Successful use of the system depends on how intelligently it is used. It is not an automatic mechanism but has to be adapted by you to the circumstances that arise. Used intelligently, it provides a logical but flexible sequence for dealing with hazards:

- you should consider all the phases of the system on the approach to every hazard, but you may not need to use every phase in a particular situation
- the information phase spans the whole system and entails a constant reassessment of plans
- if a new hazard arises consider whether you need to return to an earlier phase of the system.

Once you have learnt the system, practise it continually so that it becomes second nature.

The next section looks at how the system is applied to three of the commonest hazards: a right-hand turn, a left-hand turn and a roundabout.

Applying the system to a right-hand turn

Acceleration

Use the accelerator to maintain your speed and stability through the hazard. Depress the accelerator sufficiently to offset any loss of speed due to cornering effects.

Choose an appropriate point to accelerate smoothly away from the hazard. Take into account your speed, the road surface, the amount of turn required, other road users, and the road and traffic conditions ahead and behind.

Gear

Once you have the right speed to negotiate the hazard, select an appropriate and responsive gear for that speed.

Speed

Adjust your speed as necessary. Use the accelerator, brake or, (when necessary to avoid skidding), gears to give you the speed which will enable you to complete the manoeuvre. Make good use of acceleration sense. Know and follow the *Highway Code* advice on road junctions.

Information

Throughout this manoeuvre use your mirrors and scan to the front and sides to gather information on the position, speed and intentions of other road users. Give signals or sound your horn to benefit other road users. Remember these include pedestrians as well as cyclists, motorcyclists and drivers.

Position

Move into the appropriate position to make the manoeuvre in good time. Generally this will be towards the centre of the road, but pay attention to:

- any lane markings
- obstructions in the road
- the road surface and its condition
- the position, speed and size of other traffic – in front, behind and in the junction
- the flow of following traffic
- getting a good view
- making your intentions clear to other road users.

See Chapter 11

Applying the system to a left-hand turn

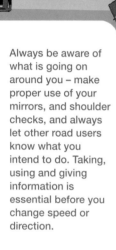

Always be aware of what is going on around you – make proper use of your mirrors, and shoulder checks, and always let other road users know what you intend to do. Taking, using and giving information is essential before you change speed or direction.

Information

Throughout this manoeuvre use your mirrors and scan to the front and sides to gather information on the position and intentions of other road users. Before starting the turn check carefully in your nearside mirror to make sure there are no road users 'trapped' on your nearside. Give signals or sound your horn to benefit other road users. Remember these include pedestrians as well as cyclists, motorcyclists and drivers.

See Chapter 10

Acceleration

Be aware of the possibility of cyclists and pedestrians moving up on your inside.

Use the accelerator to maintain your speed and stability through the hazard. Depress the accelerator sufficiently to offset any loss of speed due to cornering effects.

Taking account of your speed, the road surface, the amount of turn required, other road users, and the road and traffic conditions ahead and behind, decide whether it is appropriate to accelerate away from the hazard.

Choose an appropriate point to accelerate safely and smoothly, adjust the amount of acceleration to the circumstances.

See Chapter 10

Gear

Select an appropriate and responsive gear for the speed at which you intend to negotiate the hazard.

Speed

Adjust your speed as necessary. Use the accelerator, brake or, (when necessary to avoid skidding), gears to give you the speed which will enable you to complete the manoeuvre. Make good use of acceleration sense.

Position

Position towards the left of the road but pay attention to:

- any lane markings
- obstructions in the road
- the road surface and its condition
- the position, speed and size of other traffic – both in front and behind
- the flow of following traffic
- getting a good view
- making your intentions clear to other road users.

See Chapter 11

Applying the system to approaching a roundabout

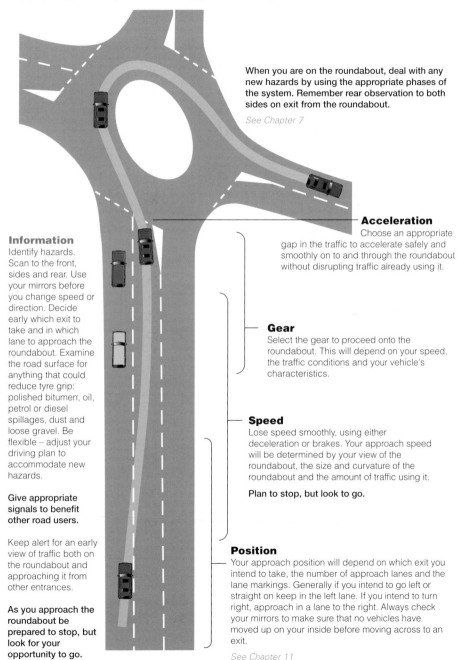

When you are on the roundabout, deal with any new hazards by using the appropriate phases of the system. Remember rear observation to both sides on exit from the roundabout.

See Chapter 7

Information

Identify hazards. Scan to the front, sides and rear. Use your mirrors before you change speed or direction. Decide early which exit to take and in which lane to approach the roundabout. Examine the road surface for anything that could reduce tyre grip: polished bitumen, oil, petrol or diesel spillages, dust and loose gravel. Be flexible – adjust your driving plan to accommodate new hazards.

Give appropriate signals to benefit other road users.

Keep alert for an early view of traffic both on the roundabout and approaching it from other entrances.

As you approach the roundabout be prepared to stop, but look for your opportunity to go.

Acceleration

Choose an appropriate gap in the traffic to accelerate safely and smoothly on to and through the roundabout without disrupting traffic already using it.

Gear

Select the gear to proceed onto the roundabout. This will depend on your speed, the traffic conditions and your vehicle's characteristics.

Speed

Lose speed smoothly, using either deceleration or brakes. Your approach speed will be determined by your view of the roundabout, the size and curvature of the roundabout and the amount of traffic using it.

Plan to stop, but look to go.

Position

Your approach position will depend on which exit you intend to take, the number of approach lanes and the lane markings. Generally if you intend to go left or straight on keep in the left lane. If you intend to turn right, approach in a lane to the right. Always check your mirrors to make sure that no vehicles have moved up on your inside before moving across to an exit.

See Chapter 11

Review

In this chapter we have looked at:

how a systematic approach to hazards can improve your driving

different types of hazard

what the system of vehicle control is and how to apply it

the importance of taking, using and giving information

using the system flexibly

7 Observation

Why you need good observation skills

'Observation' means using sight, hearing and even smell to gain as much information about conditions as possible. Effective observation is the foundation of good driving. If you do not know something is there you cannot react to it. Careful observation gives you extra time to think and react, and so gives you more control over your driving.

You may occasionally have caught yourself driving absent-mindedly. You are thinking about a number of different things, none of which have anything to do with your driving. In this state you are unprepared to deal with a sudden emergency and are quite likely to become a hazard yourself because you are not fully aware of what other road users are doing.

The *Fleetcraft* method of driving requires active attention to your driving at all times. How good you are at taking, using and giving information and applying the system of vehicle control will depend on your skills of observation and planning.

Planning

To drive safely you will have to use all the information available to form your driving plan:

• anticipate hazards

• order hazards in importance

• decide what to do.

The purpose of the plan is to put you in the right position at the right speed at the right time to negotiate hazards safely and efficiently. As soon as conditions change a new driving plan is required, so effective planning is a continual process of forming and re-forming plans.

The diagram below shows how the three key stages of planning encourage you to interpret and act on your observations:

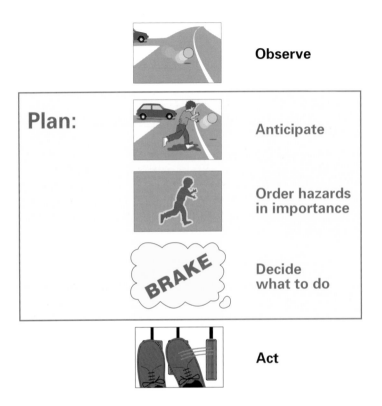

We will now look in more detail at the three stages of planning.

Anticipate

The more time that you have to react to a hazard, the more likely that you will be able to deal with it safely. Anticipating hazards gives you extra time. Your ability to anticipate depends on your training, your experience and the amount of effort you put in to developing it. A useful technique to help you develop this ability is commenting aloud (making a running commentary as you drive along on what you are observing and how you plan to deal with it).

Start with what you observe and then use your general driving experience to predict how the situation is likely to unfold: for example, your view ahead will often be obscured by vehicles or the layout of the road, yet you know from experience that hazards may be present in the unseen areas. *(See the section on observation links on pages 70-2.)* Search the road for clues which might give you added insight into likely developments. For example, when you see a ball bounce into the road you know there is a good chance that children will run after it.

Anticipating the actions of other drivers is important for your own and others' safety. It is unsafe to assume that other drivers will react correctly in any given situation. Observing someone's general progress and road behaviour will give you some idea of what sort of driver they are. Carefully observing other drivers' eye, hand and head movements will give you a better idea of their intentions, but you should always give yourself a safety margin of extra time and space to allow for others' mistakes. If you are involved in a collision, being in the right is of little consolation.

Order hazards in importance

You may see or anticipate a range of hazards at any given moment, you must then decide which is the most important. Grade the risks, and deal with them in order of importance. The importance of a hazard may change rapidly, and you must be ready to change your plans accordingly.

The intensity of danger associated with hazards varies with:

• the hazard itself

• how close it is to you

• road layout

• whether the hazard is stationary or moving

• how fast you are approaching it.

The greater the element of danger, the higher the priority that you should give it.

Decide what to do

When you have placed the hazards in order of importance, you can the decide on the best course of action. The purpose of your plan is to ensure the safety of yourself and other road users at all times. The appropriate course of action takes account of:

- what can be seen

- what cannot be seen

- what might reasonably be expected to happen

- which hazards represent the greatest threat

- what to do if things turn out differently from expected (contingency plans).

If you plan your driving you should be able to make decisions in a methodical way at any moment and without hesitation. While you are driving you should be continuously anticipating, placing hazards in order of importance and deciding what to do. At first you might find it difficult to consciously work through these three stages all the time, but with practice this will become second nature and prove a quick and reliable guide to action.

Generally things do not just happen, they take a while to develop – good planning depends on early observation and early anticipation of risk.

Throughout your next journey, aim to apply the three stages of planning:
- anticipate
- order hazards in importance
- decide what to do.

During your journey monitor your performance. How successful are you at planning? On how many occasions are you simply reacting to events rather than anticipating them?

Improving your observation skills

Below you will see a number of ways that you can improve your observational skills.

Use your eyes – scanning

Use your eyes to build up a picture of what is happening all around you, as far as you can see, in every direction. The best way to build this picture is to use your eyes in a scanning motion which sweeps the whole environment: the distance, the mid-ground, the foreground, the sides and rear. Drivers who scan the environment looking for different kinds of hazard have a lower risk of collisions than drivers who concentrate only on one area, so develop the habit of scanning repeatedly and regularly.

Scanning is a continuous process. When a new view opens out in front of you, quickly scan the new scene. By scanning the whole of the environment you will know where the areas of risk are. Check and re-check these risk areas in your visual sweeps. Avoid staring at particular risk areas because this stops you placing them in the broader context. Use all your mirrors, and consider an over the shoulder check on the occasions when it is not safe to rely on your mirrors alone – for example, when reversing, moving, joining a motorway or leaving a roundabout.

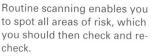
Routine scanning enables you to spot all areas of risk, which you should then check and re-check.

Peripheral vision

Peripheral vision is the area of eyesight surrounding the central area of sharply defined vision. Learn to react to your peripheral vision as well as your central vision. The eye's receptors in this area are different from the central receptors, and are particularly good at sensing movement. This helps to alert you to areas that need to be examined more closely. Peripheral vision gives you your sense of speed and lateral position, registers the movement of other road users and acts as a cue for central vision.

How speed affects observation

At 70mph the shortest distance that you can stop in is 96 metres (315 feet). This is approximately the distance between motorway marker posts). To anticipate events at this speed you need to be scanning everything between your vehicle and the horizon.

- The faster you go the further ahead you need to look. As your speed increases you need consciously to look beyond the point where your eyes naturally come to rest, to allow yourself sufficient time to react.

- Fatigue also limits your ability to see at speed. When you are tired you should slow down and consider whether to take a rest and get some fresh air.

- Speed increases the distance you travel before you can react to what you have seen, and you need to build this into your safe stopping distance.

- Your ability to take in foreground detail decreases with speed and increases as you slow down. In areas of high traffic density, such as town centres, you must slow down to be able to take in all the information necessary to drive safely.

Adjust your speed to how well you can see, the complexity of the situation and the distance it will take you to stop. You must always be able to stop within the distance you can see to be clear.

Next time you drive along a familiar route, make a mental note of the opportunities to use additional sources of information:

open spaces and breaks in hedges, fences and walls on the approach to a blind junction

the curvature of a row of trees or lamp posts

reflections in shop windows

the angle of approaching headlights

moving shadows or light cast by low sunlight or headlights

Keep your distance

Other vehicles also affect how much you can see. The closer you are to the vehicle in front the less you will be able to see beyond it, especially if it is a van or lorry. In slow-moving traffic it is better to drop back slightly so that you can see what is happening two to three vehicles in front.

When you are following a large lorry you will need to keep well back and take views to both sides of the vehicle.

On motorways it is vital to have a good view of the road ahead because of the speeds involved. Your view will depend on the curvature and gradient of the carriageway, the lane that you are in, the size and position of other vehicles and the height of your own vehicle. Allowing for these, you should keep back far enough from the vehicle in front to maintain a safe following distance. Avoid sitting in the blind spot of other vehicles by moving forward briskly or dropping back. Always check that no one is sitting in your own blind spot before you change lanes.

Weather conditions

The weather affects how far you can see, and how your vehicle performs, so it is central to your observation and driving plan. When weather conditions reduce visibility, you should reduce your speed and regularly check your actual speed on the speedometer. You should always be able to stop within the distance you can see to be clear.

Examples of weather conditions which reduce visibility are:

• fog and mist

• heavy rain

• snow and sleet

• bright sunshine.

Use of lights in bad weather

Choose your lights according to the circumstances.

• Switch on your dipped headlights when visibility is poor in daylight or fading light. This is particularly important in fog or heavy rain in daylight, when sidelights are virtually invisible.

• Generally you should use your dipped headlights whenever your wipers are in constant use.

• When there is fog or falling snow at night, foglights often give a better view than dipped headlights. Use them as an alternative to or together with dipped headlights.

• Switch off your rear foglights when you leave the fog in order not to dazzle following drivers.

• Do not use your main headlight beam when you are behind another vehicle in fog – it may dazzle the driver, and will cast a shadow of the vehicle on the fog ahead, disrupting the driver's view.

• Remember that the brilliance of rear foglights can mask the brakelights – allow more distance between you and the car in front and aim to brake gently yourself.

Using your auxiliary controls and instruments in bad weather

Make full use of your washers and wipers to keep your windscreen and rear window as clear as possible. When there is a possibility of freezing fog, put freeze-resistant screen wash in the screen wash reservoir. In fog, rain, or snow regularly check your speedometer for your actual speed. You cannot rely on your eyes to judge speed accurately in these conditions. Low visibility distorts your perception of speed.

Observing when visibility is low

When visibility is low, keep to a slow steady pace and use the edge of the carriageway, hazard lines and cat's eyes as a guide, especially when approaching a road junction or corner. Staring into featureless mist tires the eyes very quickly. Focus instead on what you can see: the vehicle in front, the edge of the road or the road ahead. Avoid fixing your focus on the tail lights of the vehicle in front because they will tend to draw you towards it. You could collide if it stopped suddenly. Be ready to use your horn to inform other road users of your presence.

Always be prepared for a sudden stop in the traffic ahead. Do not follow closely, and only overtake other traffic when you can see that it is absolutely safe to do so. This is seldom possible in fog on a two-way road. At junctions when visibility is low, wind down your window and listen for other vehicles, and consider using your horn.

Weather and the road surface

Besides affecting visibility, the weather will also affect the road surface. Snow, rain or ice will greatly reduce the grip of the tyres, making skids and aquaplaning more likely.

Be aware that special hazards exist in summer. Dust on the road reduces tyre grip. Rain may produce a slippery road surface especially after a long dry spell.

Micro climates

Look out for micro climates which can cause frost and wet patches to linger in some areas after they have disappeared elsewhere. Landscape features such as valley bottoms, shaded hillsides and shaded slopes, or large areas of shadow cast by trees or buildings can cause ice to linger and result in sudden skidding. Bridge surfaces are often colder than the surrounding roads because they are exposed on all sides, and can be icy when nearby roads are not. Patchy fog is particularly dangerous and is a common catalyst in multiple pile-ups.

Ice and wetness can linger in areas of shadow.

Adapt your driving to the weather conditions

Bad weather is often blamed for causing collisions, but the real cause is inappropriate driving for the conditions that exist. In dense fog, driving at a speed at which you can stop in the distance you can see to be clear means driving so slowly that many trips are not worthwhile. The best way to deal with a skid is not to get into it in the first place. Careful observation, the correct speed and adequate braking distances are crucial for safe driving but they are especially important in difficult weather conditions. Collisions occur when these rules are ignored.

Road surface

The type and condition of the road surface affects tyre grip and vehicle handling characteristics. Tyre grip is fundamental to driving control because it determines steering, acceleration and braking. Most drivers do not pay sufficient attention to this. Always look well ahead to identify changes in the road surface, and adjust the strength of your braking, acceleration and steering to retain adequate road holding.

Always observe the camber of the road on a curve or bend.

Surfaces which slope upwards to the inside of the curve make cornering more difficult.

Surfaces which slope downwards to the inside of the curve help cornering.

The surfaces of most roads are good for road holding when they are clean and dry. Snow, frost, ice, rain, oil, moist muddy patches, wet leaves, dry loose dust or gravel can cause tyres to lose grip. At hazards such as roundabouts or junctions, tyre deposit and diesel spillage may make the surface slippery at precisely the point where effective steering, braking and acceleration are needed to negotiate the hazard safely.

Surfacing materials	Grip characteristics	Problems
Tarmac or asphalt.	Tarmac or asphalt surfaces give a good grip when they are dressed with stones or chips.	In time they become polished and lose some of their skid resistant properties.
Concrete.	Concrete road surfaces often have roughened ribs which give a good skid resistant surface.	Some hold water, which freezes in cold weather and creates a slippery surface which is not easily seen.
Cobbles.	Low grip when wet.	Rain increases the likelihood of skidding.

Road surface irregularities

Look out for irregularities in the road surface such as potholes, projecting manhole covers, sunken gullies and bits of debris, which can damage the tyres and suspension. If you can alter your course to avoid them without endangering other traffic, do so. If you cannot, slow down to reduce shock and maintain stability as you pass over them.

Night driving

Driving at night makes observation more difficult and can reduce the amount of information available to us. As the light dwindles, your ability to see the road ahead also declines – contrast falls, colours fade and edges become indistinct.

At night your eyes need all the help you can give them. Windows, mirrors, and the lenses of lights and indicators should all be clean to give the best possible visibility. The slightest film of moisture, grease or dirt on the windows or mirrors will break up light and increase glare, making it harder to distinguish what is going on. The lights should be correctly aligned, and adjusted for the vehicle load. The bulbs should all work and the switching equipment should function properly. Windscreen washers, wipers and de-misters should also be working properly.

Lights

On unlit roads your headlights should be on main beam unless they are dipped because of other road users.

Use dipped headlights:

- in built-up areas when visibility from streetlighting is poor

- in situations when dipped headlights are more effective than the main beam, for example when going round a left-hand bend or at a hump back bridge

- in heavy rain, snow and fog when the falling droplets reflect glare from headlights on full beam.

Dip your headlights to avoid dazzling oncoming drivers, the driver in front or other road users; when you overtake another vehicle, return to full beam when you are parallel with it.

As at any time, you should drive so that you can stop in the distance that you can see to be clear; at night this distance may be limited to the area lit by your headlights. Even in the best conditions your ability to assess the speed and position of oncoming vehicles is reduced at night, so you need to allow an extra safety margin.

Dazzle

A major hazard whilst driving at night is headlight dazzle. Dazzle is caused by an intensity of the light which temporarily bleaches the retinas of your eyes. During this time you can see nothing, which is clearly dangerous.

To avoid dazzle, look towards the nearside edge of the road. This enables you to keep to your course but does not tell you what is happening in the road ahead, so slow down or stop if necessary.

Following other vehicles at night

When you follow another vehicle, dip your headlights and allow a sufficient gap so that your lights do not dazzle the driver in front. When you overtake, move out early with your headlights still dipped. If a warning is necessary you can flash your lights instead of using the horn. When you are alongside the other vehicle return to full beam. If you are overtaken, dip your headlights when the overtaking vehicle draws alongside you and keep them dipped until they can be raised without dazzling the other driver.

Information from other vehicles' lights

You can get a great deal of useful information from the front and rear lights of other vehicles; for example, the sweep of the headlights of vehicles ahead approaching a bend can indicate the sharpness of the bend, and the brakelights of vehicles in front can give you an early warning to reduce speed.

Reflective studs and markings

Reflective studs and markings are a good source of information about road layout at night. To get the most out of them you need to be familiar with the *Highway Code*. Roadside marker posts reflect your headlights and show you the direction of a curve before you can see where the actual road goes.

Cat's eyes

Cat's eyes indicate the type of white line along the centre of the road. Generally the more white paint in the line, the greater the number of cat's eyes. They are particularly helpful when it is raining at night and the glare of headlights makes it difficult to see.

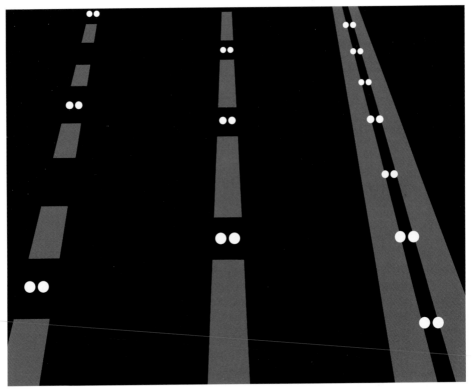

Centre lines:
one cat's eye every
other gap

Hazard lines:
one cat's eye
every gap

Double white lines:
twice as many cat's
eyes as in hazard
lines

Other ways to improve observation at night

- keep your speed down when you leave brightly lit areas to allow time for your eyes to adjust to the lower level of lighting

- any light inside the vehicle which reflects off the windows will distract you and reduce your ability to see

- certain types of spectacles – such as those with tinted lenses and those with photochromatic lenses – may be unsuitable for night driving, so check with your optician.

Night fatigue

Night driving is tiring because it puts extra strain on your eyes, and your body naturally wants to slow down as night draws on. Be aware of this problem and take appropriate action to deal with it. If you are having difficulty keeping your eyes open, you are a danger to yourself and other road users; find somewhere safe to stop, get some fresh air and rest until you are alert enough to continue safely.

Road signs and markings

Road signs and markings provide warnings about approaching hazards, and instructions and information about road use. They need to be incorporated into your driving plan as early as possible. To make the best possible use of road signs and markings you should follow the steps below.

- Observe – actively search for road signs and markings in your observation scans, and incorporate the information they give you into your driving plan. Many drivers fail to see and make use of them, and so lose valuable information.

- Understand – be able to recognise them immediately. You should be familiar with the current edition of the *Highway Code* and the *Know your Traffic Signs* book. Everyone's memory declines over time, so check your recall of road signs and markings on a regular basis.

- React – react to a sign or marking by looking ahead to what it refers to and building the information into your driving plan. Where the sign or marking refers to an unseen hazard, anticipate the hazard and adapt your plan accordingly.

Sometimes you will see several road signs on the same pole. These should generally be read from top to bottom. The nearest event is shown by the top sign, the next nearest event by the sign below that, and so on. Always be careful to use your own observations to link the signs to the road layout ahead.

Unofficial road signs

Make use of unofficial road signs such as 'Mud on Road', 'Car Boot Sale' and 'Concealed Entrance'. They provide additional information and help you anticipate the road conditions ahead.

Local road knowledge

Increasing your local knowledge of the roads can help your driving. Town driving puts heavy demands on your observation, reactions and driving skills, and you need to be alert at all times. At complicated junctions, where it is important to get into the correct lane, local knowledge is a valuable aid. But even when you know the layout of main road junctions, one-way streets, roundabouts and other local features, always plan on the basis of what you can actually see – not what usually happens. Inattentiveness is a major cause of collisions and drivers are least attentive on roads they know well. Nine out of ten collisions occur on roads that the driver is familiar with.

Making observation links

Observation links are clues to the likely behaviour of other road users. You should constantly aim to build up your own stock of observation links which will help you anticipate road and traffic conditions. Some examples follow.

When you see...	Look out for...
A cluster of lamp posts	Probable roundabout ahead.
A single lamp post on its own	The exit point of a junction.
No gap in a bank of trees ahead	Road curves to left or right.
Railway line beside road	Road will invariably go over or under it, often with sharp turns.
A pedestrian calls a cab	Cab stopping suddenly or turning or moving away from rank. Pedestrian stepping into the road.
A row of parked vehicles	Doors opening, vehicles moving off. Pedestrians stepping out from behind vehicles. Small children hidden from view.
Ice-cream vans, mobile shops, school buses, etc.	Pedestrians, especially children.
A bus at a stop	Pedestrians crossing the road to and from the bus. Bus moving off, possibly at an angle.

When you see...	Look out for...
Pedal cyclists	• Inexperienced cyclist doing something erratic. • Cyclist looking over shoulder with the intention of turning right. • Strong winds causing wobble. • Young cyclist doing something dangerous.
Fresh mud or other deposits on road. Newly mown grass, etc.	Slow-moving vehicles or animals just around the bend.
Post Office vans, trade vehicles, etc.	Points where the vehicle may stop, e.g. post box, shops, public houses, garages, building sites, etc.
Pull-ins, petrol stations, pubs, parking places, etc.	Vehicles moving in and out.
Motorway access points	Vehicles in nearside lane moving out.
Collision	Others slowing down to look.

Review

In this chapter we have looked at:

observation skills that will help to improve your driving

the link between observation, planning and acting, and the need to anticipate and order hazards in importance

scanning and using peripheral vision to get the maximum information from observation

how speed affects your vision

using additional sources of information when your view is restricted

weather conditions to watch out for and how to adjust your driving to poor visibility

ways of improving observation when you are driving at night

making full use of information from road signs and markings

increasing your skill at making observation links

Acceleration, using gears, braking and steering

Developing your skill at using the accelerator

Jerky acceleration is uncomfortable for the passengers, increases fuel consumption, puts unnecessary strains on the vehicle and adversely affects tyre grip. Learn to use the accelerator skilfully: an advanced driver will be able to operate the accelerator in a smooth and precise way.

Acceleration capability varies widely between vehicles and depends on the size of the engine, its efficiency and the power-to-weight ratio. Take time to become familiar with the acceleration capability of any vehicle you drive: the safety of many manoeuvres, particularly overtaking, depends on your good judgement of it.

Acceleration sense

Acceleration sense is the ability to vary vehicle speed in response to changing road and traffic conditions by accurate use of the accelerator. It is used in every driving situation: moving off, overtaking, complying with speed limits, following other vehicles and negotiating hazards. Good acceleration sense requires careful observation, full anticipation, sound judgement of speed and distance, driving experience and an awareness of a particular vehicle's capabilities. A lack of acceleration sense causes many common mistakes: for example, accelerating hard away from a junction and then having to brake sharply to slow to the speed of the vehicles in front; or accelerating to move up behind a slower moving vehicle and then having to brake before overtaking. If you have good acceleration sense you are able to avoid unnecessary braking.

When you have the opportunity, drive along a regular route using acceleration sense rather than braking. Notice how it improves your anticipation and increases the smoothness of the drive.

Accelerating on bends

A moving vehicle is at its most stable when its weight is evenly distributed, its engine is just pulling without increasing road speed and it is travelling in a straight line. Accelerating to increase the road speed round a bend upsets these conditions.

If you accelerate hard and alter direction at the same time you run the risk of demanding too much from the available tyre grip. If the tyres lose grip you lose steering control. To get maximum steering control, you should avoid altering your road speed at the same time.

As soon as a vehicle turns into a bend it starts to slow down and lose stability, due to cornering forces. If you maintain the same accelerator setting as you go into and round a bend you will lose road speed.

To maintain constant speed round the bend and retain stability you need to increase power by depressing the accelerator. How much to depress the accelerator is a matter of judgement but your purpose is to maintain constant speed, not to increase it. Increasing road speed on bends reduces vehicle stability.

When you need to steer and increase speed together, use the accelerator gently. Use extra care in slippery conditions or you will get wheel spin, loss of steering control and a skid.

Acceleration reduces the ability to corner because it shifts the vehicle's weight on to the back wheels and reduces front tyre grip. In front-wheel drive vehicles there is a risk of wheel spin on the front wheels because they are the driving wheels. Do not make the mistake of applying even more steering which may lead to an eventual loss of control.

Follow the guiding safety principle and adjust your speed when going round bends so that you can always stop on your own side of the road within the distance you can see to be clear.

The key points to remember are:

- select your speed for a bend according to the overall stopping distance
- maintain a constant speed round the bend
- the harder you accelerate, the less your steering ability
- use the accelerator smoothly – jerkiness causes tyre slip
- watch out for slippery surface conditions, and adjust your speed.

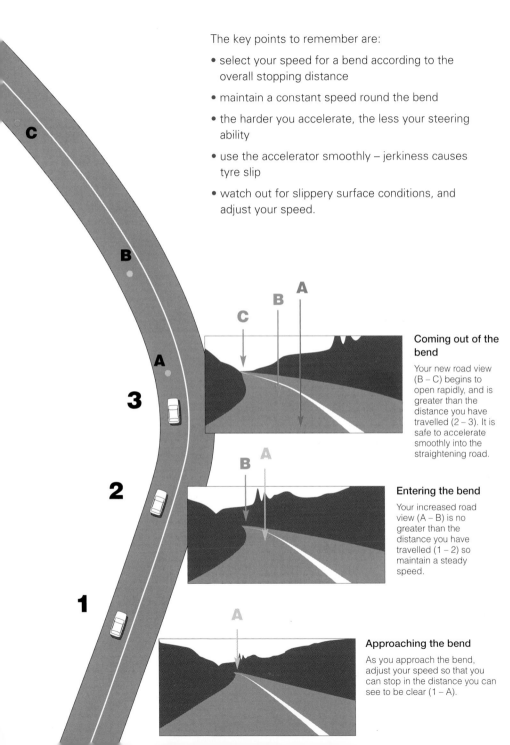

Coming out of the bend

Your new road view (B – C) begins to open rapidly, and is greater than the distance you have travelled (2 – 3). It is safe to accelerate smoothly into the straightening road.

Entering the bend

Your increased road view (A – B) is no greater than the distance you have travelled (1 – 2) so maintain a steady speed.

Approaching the bend

As you approach the bend, adjust your speed so that you can stop in the distance you can see to be clear (1 – A).

Tyre grip is not necessarily the same on each wheel. It varies with the load on the wheel and this affects how the vehicle handles. Braking, steering and accelerating alter the distribution of the load between the wheels and so affect the vehicle's balance.

Weight distribution

Steady speed	Accelerating	Braking	Cornering	Cornering and accelerating	Cornering and braking
weight is evenly distributed	weight shifts to the back	weight shifts to the front	weight shifts to the outside of the curve	weight shifts to the outside of the curve and to the back	weight shifts to the outside of the curve and to the front

Braking or accelerating as you go round a corner or bend reduces the amount of control you have over your vehicle. If more tyre grip is used for accelerating or braking, there is less available for steering and this reduces your control over the positioning of your vehicle. Eventually, if there is not enough tyre grip for steering, a skid will develop. The more slippery the road surface, the earlier this will happen. The exact outcome depends on the balance of the vehicle, and whether it has front-, back- or four-wheel drive.

Using the accelerator

Acceleration and vehicle balance

Acceleration alters the distribution of weight between the wheels of the car. When a vehicle accelerates the weight is lifted from the front and pushed down on the back wheels. During deceleration the opposite happens. This alters the relative grip of the front and rear tyres.

During acceleration

the rear tyres   the front tyres
gain grip   lose grip

During deceleration

the rear tyres   the front tyre·,
lose grip   gain grip

Acceleration affects rear-wheel drive, and most four-wheel drive vehicles, differently from front-wheel drive vehicles.

• Front-wheel drive vehicles lose grip or traction on their driving wheels because acceleration transfers weight, and therefore grip, from the front wheels to the back wheels. This reduces their ability to accelerate. In severe cases wheel spin occurs. Harsh acceleration or a slippery road surface increases the risk of wheel spin, which can be particularly dangerous when pulling out at a junction. Avoid over accelerating, and only depress the accelerator very gently in slippery conditions.

• Rear-wheel drive vehicles gain extra grip on their driving wheels, which assists acceleration (but note that excessive acceleration will cause the driving wheels to lose traction). At the same time the front is lightened.

• Four-wheel drive vehicles vary in how the power is divided between the front and back wheels, and in the type of central differential they have. The effects of acceleration therefore vary according to the model but generally four-wheel drive vehicles have good grip when accelerating.

Using the gears

Unless you are able to perfect your gear changes, your driving will always lack the finesse required of an accomplished driver. Skilful use of the gears depends on accurately matching the gear to the road speed, and using the clutch and accelerator precisely. Your vehicle can only increase speed if the engine can deliver the power.

It can only do this if you are in the right gear. You should aim to:

• be in the correct gear for every road speed and traffic situation

• make all gear changes smoothly

• engage a chosen gear without going through an intermediate gear first

• know the approximate maximum road speed for each gear of the vehicle.

These are the key points which will help you to make skilful use of the gears:

• develop good co-ordination of hand and foot movements

• recognise when to change gear by the sound of the engine

• choose the right gear for the road speed

• use the brakes rather than engine compression to slow the vehicle (except during hill descents and when there is a risk of skidding)

• brake in good time to slow to the right road speed as you approach a hazard, and then select the appropriate gear

• match engine speed to road speed before you change down.

Automatic gearboxes

An automatic gearbox allows you more time to concentrate on your driving and to keep both hands on the steering wheel for longer. You need to be familiar with and understand the manufacturer's instructions for any automatic vehicles that you drive. These are the key points to remember:

• always ensure that the footbrake is on before engaging either D or R from stationary

• do not engage D or R with a high revving engine – the choke often causes high revs.

Overlapping braking and gear changing

Sometimes it is helpful to overlap braking with the gear change. Do this by braking normally and changing the gear towards the end of braking. The advantages of this are that it takes less time and contributes to vehicle stability in certain circumstances.

These advantages have to be weighed against the disadvantage that for part of the braking period both hands are not on the steering wheel, and the possibility that the technique could lead to late, excessive braking and rushed gear changes. If you use this technique it must be properly incorporated into your planning. Braking late and rushing a gear change because of inadequate planning can destabilise your vehicle at exactly the point where you need greatest stability to negotiate the hazard.

Examples of situations where brake/gear overlap may be appropriate:

low speed turns into left and right junctions with a vehicle close behind

sharp right/left turns with a vehicle close behind

going downhill

Slowing down and stopping

You need to be able to slow down or stop your vehicle with it fully under control. The smoothness of a drive is greatly improved by early anticipation of the need to slow down or stop, and by braking gently and progressively. The ability to accurately estimate the required braking distance at different speeds and in different conditions is a central skill of safe driving, and one which you should strive to develop. There are two ways of slowing down or stopping:

• decelerating (releasing the accelerator pedal)

• using the brakes.

Deceleration

When you release the accelerator the engine slows and through engine compression exerts a retarding force on the wheels. This causes the engine to act as a brake, reducing road speed smoothly and gradually with little wear to the vehicle.

The loss of road speed is greater when you decelerate in a low gear. (This applies equally to automatic gearboxes.) Deceleration, or engine braking, provides a valuable way of losing speed on slippery roads. If the accelerator is released gently, it provides a steady and smooth braking effect in conditions where normal braking might lock the wheels – for example, on slippery roads. Engine braking is also useful on long descents in hilly country, but for normal driving it is inadequate for more than gradual variations in speed.

Using the brakes

Use the brakes if you need to make more than a gradual adjustment in road speed. You should generally keep both hands on the wheel while you brake, and plan to avoid braking on bends and corners.

Testing your brakes

Get into the habit of checking your brakes every time you use your vehicle. Check them when the vehicle is stationary before you move off, and check them again when the vehicle is moving.

- **The stationary test.** Check that the brake pedal moves freely and gives a firm positive pressure. Check that the handbrake fully secures the wheels.

- **The moving test.** Make sure that the brake system is working efficiently under running conditions. Test the footbrake as soon as possible after moving off. You only need to do this test once if you are in the same vehicle all day, provided you have no reason to suspect the performance of the brakes. Always consider the safety and convenience of other road users before you do a moving test.

Normal braking

Braking should normally be progressive and increased steadily.

Gently take up the initial free movement of the pedal

Increase the pressure progressively as required

Relax pedal pressure as unwanted road speed is lost

Release the pedal just before stopping to avoid a jerking halt

Braking reduces the grip of the rear tyres. On a bend this destabilises the balance of the vehicle.

Braking, tyre grip and balance

Braking reduces the ability to steer because of its combined effects on tyre grip and vehicle balance. Braking moves the weight of the vehicle forward on to the front wheels. This makes the steering heavier and at the same time reduces the grip of the rear tyres. On a bend this reduces stability and can cause the back wheels to lock and go into a rear wheel skid. The harsher the braking, the greater the tyre slip and the less the ability to steer. In slippery conditions harsh braking almost inevitably results in a skid.

The safe stopping distance rule

The importance of this rule for your own and other people's safety cannot be overstated. It provides a guide to the speed at which you should corner, and it indicates the speed and distance you should keep from other vehicles in all other traffic conditions. In order to practice this rule you need to be aware of:

• the braking capabilities of your vehicle

• the type and condition of the road surface – in slippery or wet conditions braking distances increase greatly

• the effects of cornering, braking and vehicle balance on tyre grip.

The only variation to this rule occurs in narrow and single track lanes where you need to allow twice the overall stopping distance that you can see to be clear. This is to allow sufficient room for any oncoming vehicle to brake also.

Overall safe stopping distance

To work out the overall safe stopping distance add thinking distance to braking distance.

Thinking distance + Braking distance = Stopping distance

- Thinking distance is the distance travelled in the time between first observing the need for action and acting. The average driver reacts to expected events in 0.7 of a second. The distance covered in that time is the same figure in feet as the speed in miles per hour; for example, at 30 mph thinking distance is 30 feet.

Never drive so fast that you cannot stop comfortably on your own side of the road within the distance you can see to be clear.

Actual thinking distance varies according to the speed of the vehicle, your physical and mental condition, your attentiveness and whether or not you are expecting something to happen. Drivers take much longer to react to unexpected events than to expected ones.

- Braking distance is the distance needed for braking in dry conditions. You should be familiar with the braking distances for different speeds recommended in the *Highway Code*.

Actual braking distance depends on the vehicle's capability, the gradient of the road and the condition of the road surface. Rising or falling gradients have a significant effect on deceleration and braking distances. Slippery surfaces greatly increase braking distances.

Do you know your safe stopping distance?

23m, 53m and 96m are the respective shortest stopping distances at 30, 50, and 70mph.

Do you know what these stopping distances actually look like on the ground? Work out your own pace length (usually less than 1m) and then pace out the three distances. Do this somewhere familiar so that you have a permanent mental image of them.

The two-second rule

One way of keeping a safe distance on fast roads between you and the vehicle in front is by leaving a gap of at least two seconds. But remember your overall stopping distance depends on your speed and the condition of the road surface. An easy way to count two seconds is to say:

[Only a fool breaks the two-second rule.]

This distance should be at least doubled in wet weather and further increased in icy conditions. If the vehicle behind you is too close, drop back further from the vehicle in front. This will allow you to brake more gently in an emergency and may prevent you being rammed from behind.

Note when the car in front passes a convenient landmark.

Count one second

Count two seconds

If you pass the object before you have counted two seconds, you are too close. Drop back and try the test again.

Braking on corners and bends

Because braking affects the balance, stability and cornering ability of vehicles, special care is needed when braking on a corner or bend:

- generally plan to avoid braking on corners because it reduces your ability to steer; if braking is necessary, apply the brakes gently and steadily

- brake in plenty of time

- adjust brake pressure according to the condition or grip of the road surface

- on steep winding descents brake firmly on the straight stretches and gently on the bends; remember to use a low gear at an early stage in the descent.

To apply the system of vehicle control you should consider your speed on the approach to a hazard and adjust it if necessary. If you need to slow down, check your mirrors, adopt the best road position and then reduce speed safely and smoothly using deceleration, braking or a combination of both.

When and how firmly you apply the brakes depends on your judgement of speed and distance. You should consider:

- your initial speed

- the road surface

- weather conditions

- the specific road and traffic conditions.

Sometimes braking may need to be firm but it should never be harsh. Harsh braking usually indicates poor observation, anticipation and planning. Aim to lose speed steadily from the first moment until you achieve the right speed to negotiate the hazard. Timing is crucial: avoid braking so early that you have to re-accelerate to reach the hazard, or so late that you have to brake forcefully.

Emergency braking on a good dry road

When braking in an emergency situation it is easy to let panic set in and apply too much pressure to the brake pedal. This will cause the wheels to lock. Once the wheels are locked all steering control will be lost. The driver must quickly decide either to brake to a standstill in a straight line if there is enough room or to relax brake pressure to regain steering control. One option is to use the cadence braking technique described below. It must be emphasised that antilock braking systems and cadence braking do not assist braking, they assist steering while braking.

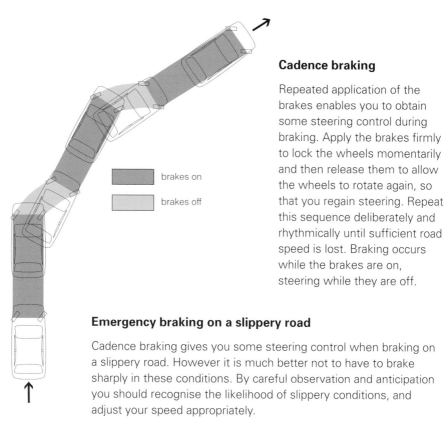

brakes on

brakes off

Cadence braking

Repeated application of the brakes enables you to obtain some steering control during braking. Apply the brakes firmly to lock the wheels momentarily and then release them to allow the wheels to rotate again, so that you regain steering. Repeat this sequence deliberately and rhythmically until sufficient road speed is lost. Braking occurs while the brakes are on, steering while they are off.

Emergency braking on a slippery road

Cadence braking gives you some steering control when braking on a slippery road. However it is much better not to have to brake sharply in these conditions. By careful observation and anticipation you should recognise the likelihood of slippery conditions, and adjust your speed appropriately.

Using the handbrake

Only use the handbrake when the vehicle is stationary. Protect the locking mechanism by pressing the release button whenever you apply or release the handbrake.

Inexperienced drivers are often taught to use the handbrake every time they come to a standstill on a journey. With experience you can judge whether it is necessary to put the handbrake on for every momentary stop.

Steering

A well-maintained vehicle travelling along a flat, straight road should hold its course with minimal steering. Camber or side winds can move the vehicle to one side but a small steering adjustment will compensate for this and keep the vehicle on a straight course. Usually you only need to make positive steering adjustments when you alter course or turn the vehicle.

Steering characteristics vary between vehicles, so make sure you are familiar with the characteristics of vehicles you drive. Some vehicles respond more than average to steering (oversteer) and others less (understeer). Power assisted steering (PAS) assists steering at slow speeds, and may cause those unfamiliar with it to oversteer.

Seat position

Good steering starts with getting your body in the right position in relation to the steering wheel. Adjust the position and angle of your seat so that you can reach the controls comfortably. You should aim for a position which allows greatest control of the steering without being uncomfortable. An uncomfortable position causes fatigue and detracts from your driving.

How to hold the steering wheel

• place your hands on the wheel with your palms on the rim at about the quarter-to-three or ten-to-two position.

- hold the wheel lightly but be ready to tighten your grip if necessary

- keep both hands on the wheel while you are driving unless it is necessary to give an arm signal or to operate a control. Always keep at least one hand on the wheel

This hold enables you to turn the wheel immediately in either direction. It is common to the majority of safe and efficient steering techniques. It is referred to in this book as the standard hold.

Make changes in direction smoothly and gradually. Make small changes in direction by turning the steering wheel without altering your hand hold.

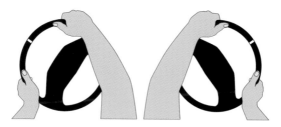

To make more positive turns, use the pull–push method described on the next page.

Pull–push

With the pull–push method neither hand passes the twelve o'clock position. Your hands remain parallel to each other on the steering wheel except when you move a hand up for the initial pull or when you make small alterations in course. One hand grips and makes the turn, the other slides round its side of the wheel ready to continue the turn. The advantage of pull–push is that it keeps both hands on the wheel and allows an immediate turn in either direction at any point during steering.

The explanation of the pull–push method given below is for a left-hand turn. For a right-hand turn follow the same method but replace left with right, and vice versa.

Start the turn with a pull and not a push because it gives better control.

Slide the left hand up to a higher position on the wheel, but not past the twelve o'clock point.

Pull the wheel down with the left hand.

As the left hand pulls down, slide the right hand down, allowing the rim to slide through the right hand fingers. Keep the right hand level with the left hand until it nears the bottom of the wheel.

If more turn to the left is necessary start pushing up with the right hand and at the same time slide the left hand up the wheel, keeping it level with the right.

Repeat these movements until sufficient turn is obtained, feeding the wheel back through the hands with similar but opposite movements to those used for the turn. Do not let the wheel spin back on its own.

In certain circumstances, for example during skidding or during very slow or high speed manoeuvres, it may be advantageous to use a different technique from pull–push.

Rotational steering

Hold the wheel using the standard hold described on page 86. The quarter-to-three position allows the greatest degree of turn without having to reposition a hand.

Most alterations to course (up to about 120 degrees of steering wheel turn) can be made by turning the wheel while keeping a light but fixed hand hold.

For more acute bends (requiring more than about 120 degrees of steering wheel turn) reposition your lower hand at 12 o'clock and continue smoothly pulling down the wheel.

When you can see that a bend is going to require more than 120 degrees of steering wheel turn, place your leading hand at the top of the wheel before starting the turn.

When you steer do you start with a pull rather than a push? If in the past you have tended to start with a push, practise pulling first. Notice how it contributes to the smoothness and control of your steering.

If even more turn is required, place your other hand near the top of the wheel to continue the turning motion.

Straighten the wheel by using a similar series of movements but in the opposite direction. Although the self-centring action of the wheel assists the return, you must keep it under control.

Manoeuvring at slow speeds and in confined spaces

Manoeuvring in a confined space sometimes requires rapid movements of the steering wheel. Generally the standard pull–push technique provides effective steering, but on occasions, especially when reversing, other hand holds may give better control.

Avoid the temptation to turn the steering wheel while the vehicle is stationary. It damages the tyres and puts excessive strain on the steering linkages, particularly in vehicles with power assisted steering. Only turn the steering wheel when the vehicle is moving, even if it is only moving very slowly.

Reversing hold

Put one hand at the top of the steering wheel and use this hand to move the wheel. Use the other hand to hold the wheel low down, either loosely while the wheel slides through or tightly when you take a new grip at the top. Look in your mirrors and over your shoulders to get a clear view. You can improve your view to the left by putting your left arm on the back of the seat. If the seat belt restricts your movement, release it but do not forget to put it back on.

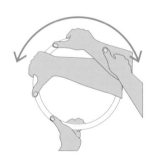

Advice on reversing

Reversing can be difficult, especially in a confined area. The faster it is done the more difficult it is to control, so always reverse slowly. Before you reverse:

• scan the area for suitability and obstructions

• ensure you have an unobstructed view

• use mirrors to advantage whilst reversing but do not be totally reliant on them

• wind down your door window to give you more all round awareness

• get someone to help you if possible.

While reversing:

- travel slowly and slip the clutch if necessary – in automatic vehicles you can check the speed by using the left foot on the brake

- remember that, as you steer, the front of your vehicle moves out and could strike nearby objects

- look all round you to make sure there are no hazards.

If your reversing lights fail use your indicator lights or brake-lights to light the area behind you when it is dark, but be careful not to mislead other road users.

Steering guidelines

These are the key points to remember for effective steering:

- do not place your elbows on the window frame or arm rests because this reduces control

- place your hands on the wheel in the ten-to-two or quarter-to-three position: only grip tightly when you need to exert maximum effort

- keep both hands on the wheel when cornering, braking firmly or driving through deep surface water

- on slippery roads steer as delicately as possible or you may skid.

Good steering requires good observation, anticipation and planning. If the brakes are applied sharply or if the speed is too high, steering cannot be precise.

Review

In this chapter we have looked at:

improving your skill in using the basic controls for moving and stopping a vehicle

how to get the maximum safety out of the tyre grip available on your vehicle

how acceleration and braking affect vehicle balance

why it is important to match engine speed to road speed when you change gear

how to use the gears in different circumstances

testing your brakes

why stopping distance is so important, and how to assess safe braking distances

how to use your steering to give you the greatest safety and control

9 Skidding

Avoiding skidding

What causes a skid? Many people when asked this question would say that it was the result of poor road or weather conditions, but this is not really true. A skid does not just happen – it is almost always the result of a driver's actions. It is often caused by altering course or speed too harshly for the road conditions.

You should aim to drive and control a vehicle in such a way that it does not skid. This becomes more difficult when road or weather conditions deteriorate, but by using your skills of observation, anticipation and planning you can do a lot to minimise the risks of skidding.

First you need to understand how a skid happens, what warning signs to look out for and what actions to avoid.

How does a skid happen?

A vehicle skids when one or more of the tyres loses normal grip on the road, causing an involuntary movement of the vehicle. This happens when the grip of tyres on the road becomes less than the force or forces acting on the vehicle. The following illustrations explain what these forces are.

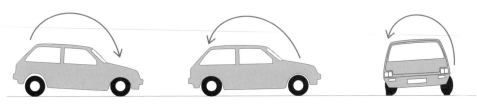

Braking   Accelerating   Cornering

These forces act on a vehicle whenever you operate the controls – the brake, the accelerator, the clutch or the steering wheel. If you brake or accelerate while steering round a bend or corner, two forces are combined. As we saw in Chapter 8 page 76, there is only limited tyre grip available and if these forces become too powerful they break the grip of the tyres on the road. You should never drive to the limits of the tyre grip available – always leave a safety margin to allow for the unforeseen.

Skidding is usually the result of driving too fast for the conditions. This creates the circumstances from which a skid can develop. If a driver suddenly or forcibly accelerates, brakes, releases the clutch without matching engine speed to road speed or changes direction, this may cause wheel spin. On a slippery road surface, it takes much less force to break the grip of the tyres.

If you have ever experienced a skid, you will probably remember that you were changing either the speed or direction of the vehicle – or both – just before the skid developed.

Causes of skidding

The commonest causes of skidding are:

• excessive speed for the circumstances

• coarse steering in relation to a speed which is not itself excessive

• harsh acceleration

• sudden or excessive braking.

When a skid develops, the driver's first action should be to remove the cause. Later in this section we shall discuss the causes of skidding and how to remove them in more detail.

Antilock braking systems (ABS)

An increasing number of vehicles are fitted with an automatic antilock braking system (ABS). The purpose of an antilock braking system is to retain steering control during harsh or emergency braking.

The system is designed to sense the slowing down of the wheels and to release them before they lock up fully. It reapplies the brakes once the wheels start to rotate again. Once ABS is activated, the driver has to maintain maximum pressure on the brake pedal throughout.

This means that in principle the wheels should never lock, but on a slippery surface the wheels may not rotate immediately after the ABS system releases the wheel, allowing momentary lock-up. ABS is a sophisticated safety device, however it does not increase the grip of the tyres on the road, nor can it prevent certain types of skidding. In some circumstances a vehicle equipped with ABS can stop within a shorter distance than if the wheels were locked, but it does not reduce, and could increase, the stopping distance on a slippery surface. If you activate the antilock braking system, this suggests that you are not driving within safe limits.

Traction control systems

Traction control improves steering and vehicle stability by controlling excess wheel slip on individual wheels. It also reduces engine power when there is excessive wheel slip, allowing the wheels to regain traction (or grip) and stability. It allows the vehicle to make maximum use of tyre grip, especially on slippery surfaces and where the friction of the road surface is uneven (for example, where one wheel is on a normal surface and the other on ice or snow).

The technique of skid control is fundamentally different in a vehicle fitted with traction control. Different manufacturers use different systems of traction control, so if your vehicle has traction control you must consult your vehicle handbook and follow the manufacturer's advice on what to do in skid situations.

Observe – weather and road conditions to watch for

Skidding is more likely in bad weather conditions and on slippery road surfaces. These are some of the obvious and less obvious hazards you need to watch out for:

- snow, ice, frost, heavy rain
- wet mud, damp leaves or oil, which can create sudden slippery patches on the road surface
- cold spots in shaded areas, under trees, on slopes or hills – watch how other vehicles behave in icy weather
- dry loose dust or gravel
- a shower or rain after a long dry spell – accumulated rubber dust and oil mixed with water can create a very slippery surface

- worn road surfaces that have become polished smooth
- concrete, which usually provides good grip, but which may hold surface water and become slippery in freezing weather
- cobbled roads, still found in some towns and cities, which become very slippery when wet
- changes in the road surface on bridges, which may be more slippery than the surrounding roads.

The risks of these hazards are accentuated at corners and junctions because you are more likely to combine braking, accelerating and steering in these situations.

Anticipate and plan – adjust your driving to the road conditions

Good road observation will help you to evaluate poor weather and road conditions accurately and adjust your speed accordingly:

- leave plenty of room for manoeuvre, reduce your speed and increase the distance you allow for stopping to match the road conditions – on a slippery surface a vehicle can take many times the normal distance to stop
- use a higher gear in slippery conditions to avoid wheel spin, especially when moving off or travelling at low speeds
- on a slippery surface aim to brake, steer and change gear as smoothly as possible, so that the grip of the tyres is not broken.

Care of the vehicle

Most skids are the result of how a vehicle is driven, but keeping your vehicle in good condition helps to minimise the risk of skidding:

- tyres should be correctly inflated and have adequate tread depth – check tyre treads and tyre pressure regularly
- defective brakes and faulty suspension are especially dangerous on slippery surfaces and may help to cause or aggravate a skid – do not increase the risk by neglecting these problems.

Correcting different types of skid

The action you take to correct a skid depends on what type of skid it is. The illustrations which follow show how to recognise and correct a rear wheel, front wheel and four wheel skid.

Correcting a rear wheel skid

In a rear wheel skid you feel the back of the vehicle swing out – on a corner or bend the swing is always to the outside of the curve. In many situations, removing the cause will quickly correct the skid without having to alter the steering. But if the speed of the vehicle is excessive there may not be sufficient space to regain directional control whatever you do.

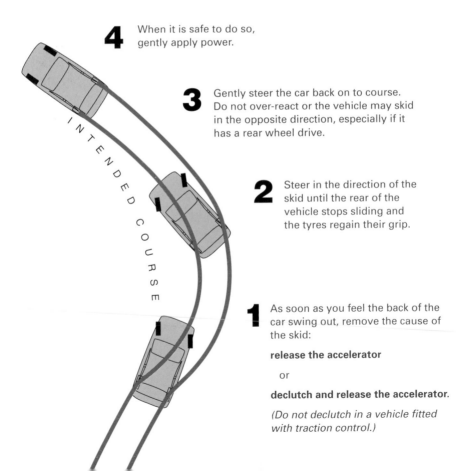

4 When it is safe to do so, gently apply power.

3 Gently steer the car back on to course. Do not over-react or the vehicle may skid in the opposite direction, especially if it has a rear wheel drive.

2 Steer in the direction of the skid until the rear of the vehicle stops sliding and the tyres regain their grip.

1 As soon as you feel the back of the car swing out, remove the cause of the skid:

release the accelerator

or

declutch and release the accelerator.

(Do not declutch in a vehicle fitted with traction control.)

INTENDED COURSE

Correcting a front wheel skid

In a front wheel skid you feel the front of the vehicle carry straight on when you are expecting it to steer left or right. In many situations, removing the cause will quickly correct the skid without having to alter the steering. But if the speed of the vehicle is excessive there may not be sufficient space to regain directional control whatever you do.

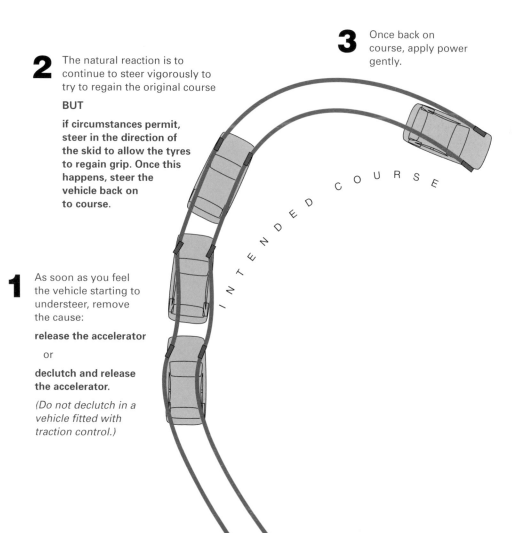

3 Once back on course, apply power gently.

2 The natural reaction is to continue to steer vigorously to try to regain the original course

BUT

if circumstances permit, steer in the direction of the skid to allow the tyres to regain grip. Once this happens, steer the vehicle back on to course.

1 As soon as you feel the vehicle starting to understeer, remove the cause:

release the accelerator

or

declutch and release the accelerator.

(Do not declutch in a vehicle fitted with traction control.)

INTENDED COURSE

Correcting a four wheel skid

In a four wheel skid – usually the result of excessive or sudden braking causing all four wheels to lose grip on the road – you feel a lightness and loss of direction as all four wheels lock up and the vehicle begins to slide. This is most likely where the driver has had to lose speed rapidly in an emergency. Excessive speed is often a contributory cause.

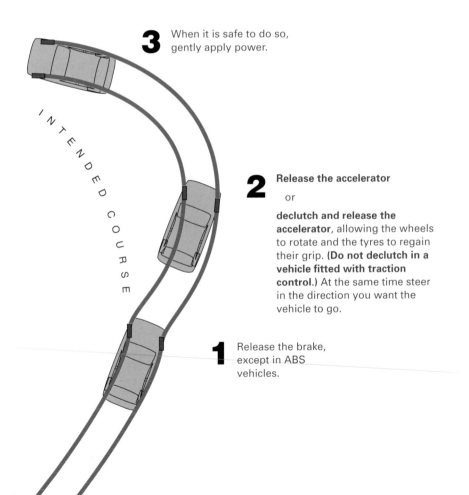

3 When it is safe to do so, gently apply power.

INTENDED COURSE

2 Release the accelerator

or

declutch and release the accelerator, allowing the wheels to rotate and the tyres to regain their grip. (**Do not declutch in a vehicle fitted with traction control.**) At the same time steer in the direction you want the vehicle to go.

1 Release the brake, except in ABS vehicles.

Cadence braking
(rhythm braking, pumping the brakes)

The following discussion is only applicable to vehicles not fitted with ABS.

If you brake hard in wet or slippery conditions it is likely that your road wheels will lock and you will lose steering control. Your vehicle will skid in a straight line and you may well collide with something before the skid ends.

If it is necessary to alter course to avoid a collision, you can only regain steering control by allowing the wheels to rotate. Vehicles fitted with ABS do this automatically, but in non-ABS vehicles the greatest degree of control is gained by pumping the brakes rhythmically. Brakes are most effective when they are on the point of locking up, so each time the brake is pumped hard, maximum braking effect takes place. When the brakes are released the wheels rotate and steering control is regained. Cadence braking therefore gives you a combination of braking and steering effect – braking while the brakes are on, steering while they are off.

Pump the brakes with a deliberate movement, pausing momentarily at the full extent of brake pedal travel – avoid bouncing the foot on and off the pedal.

Training in skid correction

Skid correction training can help to:

• raise your standard of driving

• give you confidence in driving under any conditions

• equip you to meet any emergency which might arise.

There are organisations which provide instruction on skidding for members of the public. It is usually given on a skid pan or in a specially designed skid car which can simulate different loss of control situations.

Review

In this chapter we have looked at:

the forces on a vehicle which can break the grip of the tyres on the road

how a driver's actions can cause a skid

reducing the risks of skidding by observing, anticipating, and planning – and by maintaining your vehicle in a good condition

how to recognise and remove the cause of a skid

what a front wheel, rear wheel or four wheel skid feels like and how to correct each type

variations in the characteristics of vehicles with different types of drive

using the technique of pumping the brakes to gain directional control

antilock braking systems and how they work

how to find out about practical skidding instruction.

10 Driver's Signals

The purpose of signals

The purpose of signals is to inform other road users of your presence or intentions.

Signals are used to give information, so they must be given clearly, in good time and in accordance with the methods illustrated in the *Highway Code*. As with any communication, signals can easily be misinterpreted. Always make the meaning of your signals clear. Other road users use your position and speed to interpret what your signals mean, so be aware of this, especially when safety or other considerations cause you to take an unusual position. These are the key points to remember:

• the need to give a signal on the approach to every hazard, and before you change direction or speed

• remember that signalling does not give you any special right to carry out the actions you indicate

• follow the *Highway Code* – check your mirrors before you signal or manoeuvre.

Avoid confusion

As well as taking care that your own signals are not misleading, you also need to be cautious about how you interpret the signals of other road users. For example, does a vehicle flashing the left-hand indicator mean that the driver intends to:

• park the vehicle, possibly immediately after a left-hand junction?

• turn into a left-hand junction?

• carry straight on, having forgotten to cancel the last signal?

In practice you should use the position and speed of the vehicle to interpret what the driver intends.

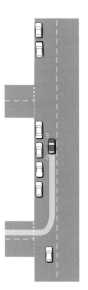

The range of signals

The signals available to you are:

- indicators
- horn signals
- hazard warning lights
- brakelights
- headlights
- arm signals
- courtesy signals (for example, raising a hand to thank another driver).

On the following pages we look at how you can make best use of these signals, each of which has its advantages and disadvantages. Where there is a choice, consider which signal is likely to be the most effective.

Using the indicators

You should give a signal for each manoeuvre you intend to carry out. One signal should not cover two manoeuvres. Use your indicators in accordance with the *Highway Code*, but bear in mind the following points.

- A signal to indicate that you are going to turn left and a signal to indicate that you intend to pull into the side of the road and stop can easily be confused by other road users. If there is a possibility of causing confusion, take steps to avoid it. Consider giving an arm signal to clarify your intentions. Be particularly careful if you intend to park just past a left-hand junction, especially if a vehicle is waiting to emerge.

- Use your position to make your intentions clear to other road users. If you cannot use your road position, or if you think it necessary, reinforce your indicator signal with an arm signal. For example, you indicate to turn right but a parked vehicle causes you to move to the centre of the road just before the junction. Other drivers may think you have indicated to warn of your intention to move out to pass the parked vehicle. Adding an arm signal makes it clear that you intend to turn right.

Cancelling indicator signals

Leaving an indicator working after a turn has been completed confuses other drivers and can easily cause a collision. Do not accept an indicator signal as complete proof of another driver's intention.

Sometimes the self-cancelling mechanisms do not work, especially when a turn is followed by a bend in the same direction. Take care to cancel the indicator yourself in such situations.

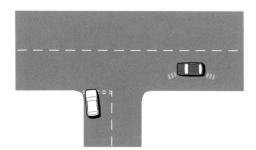

Do not accept an indicator signal as complete proof of another driver's intention.

Using the horn

Sound your horn when it could benefit pedestrians and other road users in situations where they may not have noticed you or cannot see you.

You should consider using the horn on the approach to any hazard. When you decide it is necessary to sound the horn, alter your position or speed so that you can stop if there is no reaction to your warning. Do not use the horn to challenge or rebuke other road users. Be aware that some people, especially children, the elderly and those with a hearing disability may not hear a horn.

These are the key points to remember:

• first alter your position to avoid the hazard and consider reducing your speed, then sound the horn to inform the other road user(s)

• use your horn in good time

• adjust the length of the horn note to the circumstances

• using the horn does not justify using excessive speed for the circumstances (for example, when driving round a blind bend).

These are examples of circumstances where it could be beneficial to use the horn:

to attract the attention of another road user who is obviously vulnerable (pedestrians and cyclists – especially children – are most at risk)

to inform the driver in front of your presence before you overtake

when you approach a hazard where the view is very limited – for example, a blind bend or hump back bridge

to warn the occupants of parked vehicles that you are about to pass them

Using hazard warning lights

Only use hazard lights to alert other drivers to your presence when you have stopped. Do not use hazard lights when moving except on unrestricted dual carriageways and motorways. Here you can use hazard lights briefly to warn the vehicles behind that there is a hold-up.

Using brakelights

Brakelights are used to indicate either slowing down or your intention to stop. Remember to check in your mirrors before using your brakes.

- use your brakelights as an early indication of your intention to slow down. Lightly touch your brakes, well in advance of the anticipated hazard, to alert the driver behind to your intention. This is especially useful when the driver behind is too close

- remember that rear foglights are brighter than brakelights and may mask them when you are slowing down.

Flashing your headlights

Use headlight flashes when the horn would not be heard, and in place of the horn at night. Headlight flashes should only be used for one purpose: to inform other road users that you are there. Never assume that a headlight flash from another driver is a signal to proceed. Use a headlight flash in the daylight to:

- alert other drivers to your presence when you are approaching from behind.

Use your judgement to decide the duration of the flash and how far in advance you should give it. This is critical and will depend on your speed. The purpose of the flash is to inform the driver in front of your presence, not that you intend to overtake. It does not give you the right to overtake. Use it when speed makes it likely that the horn would not be heard.

During darkness use headlight flashes to inform other road users of your presence:

- on the approach to a hill crest or narrow hump back bridge

- when travelling along very narrow, winding roads

- before overtaking another vehicle – flash your headlights early enough to enable the driver of the other vehicle to react to them.

Do not give these signals when they might be misunderstood by road users for whom they are not intended.

Using arm signals

Although arm signals are no longer in regular use, you should know what they mean and how to give them in accordance with the *Highway Code*. The general under-use of arm signals makes them stand out, and other road users are more likely to notice them.

Arm signals are especially useful in reinforcing other signals in ambiguous situations. Common situations where they could be useful are:

to reinforce a right-hand turn indicator in an unclear situation

to reinforce brakelights on the approach to a pedestrian crossing

Do not use arm signals when you need both hands on the steering wheel to control the car, such as during heavy braking at speed or sharp cornering.

Using courtesy signals

Courtesy signals are important because they encourage cooperative use of the road space and promote road safety. Acknowledging the courtesy of other road users encourages good driving and helps you to develop a positive attitude to driving. Using a courtesy signal to apologise or defuse a potential conflict can make a real difference to road safety. Use courtesy signals:

• to thank another driver for letting you go first

• to apologise when you have unintentionally caused inconvenience.

Use either hand to give a courtesy signal but not at the risk of your steering control. You can signal without removing your hand from the wheel by raising your palm or nodding your head.

Responding to other people's signals

Signals other than those given by authorised officials should be treated with caution. If someone beckons you to move forward, always check for yourself whether it is safe to do so.

Review

In this chapter we have looked at:

the place of signals in the system of vehicle control

why it is important to give signals clearly

the different signals available to you, and how and when to use them

how courtesy signals can contribute to road safety

11 Positioning

The ideal road position depends on many things: safety, observation, traffic conditions, road layout, cornering, manoeuvrability, assisting traffic flow and making your intentions clear. The overriding consideration is safety, which should never be sacrificed for any other advantage. In so far as there is a standard position on the road, it is the one which gives you the best view but with careful regard to safety.

Zones of different risk

Position is critical to safety. By carefully choosing your position you can do much to reduce the risk of having a collision. Think of the road as zones of different risk. To the nearside there is a risk of coming into conflict with cyclists and pedestrians (especially children), and parked vehicles and their occupants. To the offside, there is a risk of coming into conflict with oncoming vehicles. Between the two extremes there is a relatively safe zone in which to progress. This is towards the left of the centre of the road, giving sufficient clearance to pedestrians and other nearside hazards.

This is only a very general area of safety and you must adapt your position to the actual circumstances.

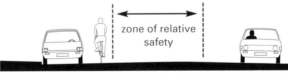

zone of relative safety

In choosing your road position never sacrifice safety for any other advantage.

Positioning on the approach to hazards

The system of vehicle control provides a safe and methodical approach to hazards. Part of this approach is an awareness of the likely risks involved. This section describes the factors you should take into account as you position your vehicle to approach and pass hazards.

As you approach a hazard you need to be aware that risks can arise from the sides of the road. Dangers can come from anywhere but you will generally have less time to react to hazards coming from the nearside. In narrow roads and one-way systems you need to be equally attentive to both sides of the road.

Roadside hazards

Common roadside hazards that you should be aware of are:
- pedestrians, especially children, stepping off the footpath
- parked vehicles and their occupants
- cyclists, especially children
- concealed junctions.

If you identify hazards on the nearside, steer a course closer to the crown of the road. This has two benefits:
- it gives you a better view
- it provides more space in which to take avoiding action should this become necessary.

If oncoming traffic makes it unsafe to adopt this position or if the road is too narrow, reduce your speed. There is an important trade-off between your speed and the clearance around your vehicle. The less space you have the slower you should go.

If traffic conditions allow, a course closer to the crown of the road gives you a better view and provides more space in which to take avoiding action.

When you drive along a row of parked vehicles get into the habit of asking yourself 'Could I stop in time if a child ran out?'

Keep as far from rows of parked vehicles as the circumstances allow. There is always the possibility that a pedestrian, especially a child, might run out from between them, or that an occupant might suddenly step out into your path. If traffic or road conditions prevent you from moving out, slow down. A good rule of thumb is to try to give at least an open door's clearance to the side of any parked vehicles.

Improving the view into nearside road junctions

Position yourself so that you can see as much of the road ahead as possible and so that other road users can see you. You can improve your view into nearside roads by positioning your vehicle towards the crown of the road. This also makes you more visible to vehicles pulling out from nearside junctions. You must, however, take into account any vehicles on your offside. Adopt a position that minimises the overall danger from both sides of the road.

Following position

In a stream of traffic, always keep a safe distance behind the vehicle in front. When following a vehicle, remember to adopt the 2 second rule. If the surface is wet this should be doubled.

These are some of the advantages of keeping your distance from the vehicle in front:

- you have a good view, and can increase it along both sides by slight changes of position – this enables you to be fully aware of what is happening on the road ahead
- you can stop your vehicle safely if the driver in front brakes firmly without warning
- you can extend your braking

In this illustration the driver is following too closely to the vehicle in front. The aerial plan shows how hazards in the shaded area cannot be seen.

In this illustration the driver is keeping a good safe position and all the hazards are visible. This view could be improved by moving slightly to the nearside or offside.

distance so that the driver behind has more time to react

- you can see when it is safe to move up into the overtaking position.

Overtaking position

When you can see that there are no hazards ahead and you have identified an opportunity to overtake, you should move into the overtaking position. This is closer to the vehicle in front than the following position and you should only use it in readiness for overtaking. If an observed or anticipated hazard comes into view you must move back to a safe following distance from the vehicle in front.

As you move closer to the vehicle in front the driver is likely to realise that you want to overtake. You must be careful not to intimidate the other driver or to appear aggressive by following too closely. Such misunderstandings are dangerous and counter-productive. They can cause the other driver to speed up, making it more difficult to overtake.

Position for turning

Your position for turning depends on the other traffic, the road layout, the position of any obstacles and the effect of these obstacles on traffic behaviour. Generally the best position on the approach to the junction where you are going to turn is on the nearside of the road for a left turn and towards the centre line for a right turn.

If you intend to turn right and oncoming traffic is encroaching on your side of the road, move away from the centre line.

Give careful consideration to:

traffic light filter arrows

carriageway markings

other traffic

obstructions

If you intend to turn left and the corner has a sharp angle, or is obscured, or pedestrians are present, approach the corner from further out than normal. Avoid 'swan necking', which is approaching close to the nearside and then swinging out to the right just before turning left into the junction.

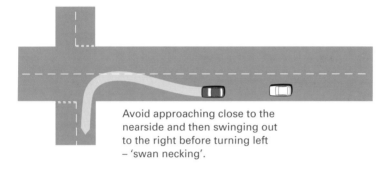

Avoid approaching close to the nearside and then swinging out to the right before turning left – 'swan necking'.

Crossroads

The *Highway Code* advises that two vehicles turning across each other at a crossroads should pass each other offside to offside.

Passing offside to offside

Position for stopping behind other vehicles

Before you come to a stop think about your next move. Position your vehicle so that you can continue with minimum inconvenience to yourself and other road users.

When you stop behind a line of vehicles and there is no one following, consider stopping well short of the vehicle in front and watch for traffic coming up behind. If an approaching vehicle appears to have left braking too late, move forward to allow it extra space to stop in. An example of this is where there are traffic lights at a roadworks close to a bend. You should consider stopping in the bend so that the drivers of following vehicles can see you as they approach the bend.

Parking

Park your vehicle safely: do not leave it where it can cause inconvenience or danger to others. If you park on a hill, put the vehicle in a low gear and consider turning your wheels into the kerb.

Leave yourself sufficient room to pull out and pass the vehicle in front if necessary.

A good rule of thumb for judging this distance is to stop so that you can see the rear tyres of the vehicle in front.

Review

In this chapter we have looked at:

the overriding importance of safety in choosing a road position

why a position towards the centre of the road is relatively risk free

common roadside hazards that you need to be aware of

where to position your vehicle if nearside hazards are present

where to position your vehicle while following a vehicle in front

how to position your vehicle for turning and stopping

how to turn past another vehicle at a crossroads

12 Cornering

The system of vehicle control – principles for safe cornering

Cornering is potentially dangerous so you should use the system of vehicle control to help you carry out the manoeuvre safely. Correctly assessing the severity of the bend is essential for safety. Applying the system and the safe stopping rule gives us four key principles of safe cornering:

• your vehicle should be in the right position on the approach

• you should be travelling at the right speed for the corner or bend

• you should have the right gear for that speed

• you should be able to stop on your own side of the road in the distance you can see to be clear.

Applying these principles to the variations in bend, traffic conditions, road surface conditions, visibility and other factors requires good judgement and planning. But before we look in more detail at using the system of vehicle control for cornering, it will be helpful to consider the other key factors that affect a vehicle's ability to corner safely.

Cornering effects

A moving vehicle is at its most stable when travelling in a straight line on a level course and at constant speed. It will continue to travel on a straight course unless you apply some other force to alter its direction. When you steer, the turning force to alter direction comes from the action of the front tyres on the road. If the front tyre grip is broken, the car will continue in a straight line. On tighter bends, at higher speeds and in heavier vehicles, the demands on tyre grip are greater.

As you corner, your body feels as if it is being pushed out towards the side of the car. In fact it is continuing to move in a straight line and only turns into the bend because it is forced to by the car. Tyre grip faces competing demands from three forces:

- steering

- accelerating

- braking.

The more you brake or accelerate the less tyre grip you have for steering. The faster you go into a corner or bend, the greater the tyre grip required to keep you on course round it.

The practical outcome of these forces is to cause vehicles to continue in a straight line rather than turning whenever tyre grip is lost.

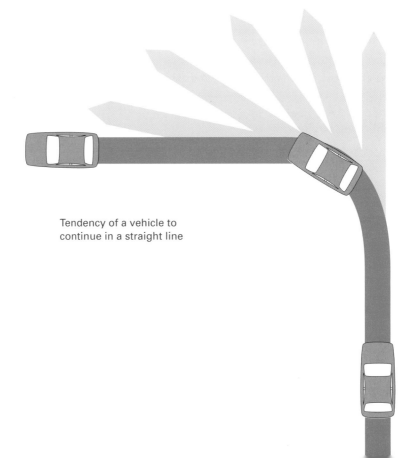

Tendency of a vehicle to
continue in a straight line

Vehicle characteristics

Roadworthiness

Vehicles vary in their ability to corner, and they only corner to the best of their ability if they are well maintained. Steering, suspension, shock absorbers, tyres, tyre pressures and the loading of the vehicle all affect its balance and road grip when cornering. Make sure that your vehicle and tyres are in good condition and that your tyre pressures are kept at the recommended levels. Also position loads so that they do not upset the balance of the vehicle.

Vehicle specification

The specifications that affect the handling characteristics of a vehicle are:

• the type of drive (front-wheel, rear-wheel or four-wheel)

• suspension and damping

• traction control, if fitted

• adaptive suspension, if fitted

• the drive ratio and central differential characteristics on a four-wheel drive vehicle.

Understeer and oversteer

Understeer is the tendency of a vehicle to turn less, and oversteer is the tendency of a vehicle to turn more in response to a given turn of the steering wheel. The tendency to understeer or oversteer is a characteristic of the vehicle itself and depends primarily on what sort of drive the vehicle has. In general, front-wheel drive vehicles understeer and rear-wheel drive vehicles oversteer. Make a point of knowing whether your vehicle understeers or oversteers and adapt your driving to the characteristics of your vehicle on corners and bends.

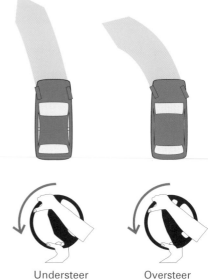

Understeer   Oversteer

In a front-wheel drive car, you will increase understeer if you:

• enter the bend at too high a speed

• apply power in the bend

• steer too sharply.

You can reduce this understeer by partially reducing power and/or steering. But if power is reduced by too much too suddenly, you may convert the understeer to oversteer.

A rear-wheel drive car initially behaves in the same way, but if excessive power is applied on a slippery surface the understeer may convert quite suddenly to oversteer. This requires a prompt steering correction in the opposite direction to the bend.

Four-wheel drive cars provide better road adhesion all round but when driven to extremes they will behave in a similar way to the front- or rear-wheel drive model from which they are derived.

Camber and superelevation

The road surface is not normally level across its width but is built with a slope to assist drainage. The slope across the road affects steering. The normal slope falls from the crown of the road to the edges and is called camber:

• on a left-hand bend camber increases the effect of your steering because the road slopes down in the direction of turn

• on a right-hand bend camber reduces the effect of steering because the road slopes away from the direction of turn.

This only applies if you keep to your own side of the road. If you cross over the crown to the other side of the road, camber will have the opposite effect on steering.

There are many instances, especially at junctions, where the slope across the road surface is at an unexpected angle. Whatever the slope, if it falls in the direction of your turn it will increase the effect of your steering; if it rises in the direction of your turn it will reduce the effect of your steering. You need to consider the slope across the road when deciding on your speed for a bend.

Superelevation is where the whole width of the road is banked up towards the outside edge of the bend, making the slope favourable for cornering in both directions.

Crown camber

Superelevation

Summary of factors affecting cornering

To sum up, the factors that determine your vehicle's ability to corner are:

- speed
- the amount of steering you apply
- the amount of acceleration and/or braking
- the characteristics of the vehicle
- the slope across the road surface – camber and superelevation
- the road surface and how the weather has affected its grip.

The system of vehicle control and the limit point

Now that you can identify the factors which affect your vehicle's ability to corner, the following section explains in detail how to use the system of vehicle control and the limit point to corner safely.

The system of vehicle control assists planning in approaching and negotiating corners and bends. The five phases of the system –

information, position, speed, gear and acceleration – highlight the essential factors that you must consider when cornering.

As you approach a bend using the system you should be seeking as much information as possible about the severity of the bend. You should use all the observational aids and clues available to you (weather, road surface, road signs, road markings, the line made by lamp posts and trees, the speed and position of oncoming traffic, the angle of headlights at night, etc.) to anticipate and plan for the severity of the bend. A valuable aid to observation is the limit point because it gives you a systematic way of judging the correct speed through the bend.

How to use the limit point to help you corner

The limit point is the furthest point along a road to which you have an uninterrupted view of the road surface. On a level stretch of road this will be where the right-hand side of the road appears to intersect with the left-hand side of the road. This point of intersection is known as the limit point. To drive safely you must be able to stop on your own side of the road within the distance you can see to be clear – that is, the distance between you and the limit point.

The ability to stop on your own side of the road in the distance you can see to be clear determines how fast you can go. The more distant the limit point the faster you can go because you have more space to stop in. The closer the limit point the slower you must go because you have less space to stop in.

As you approach and go through a bend the limit point appears at first to remain stationary as you approach it, then to move away at a constant speed and finally to sprint away to the horizon as you come out of the bend. The technique of limit point analysis is to match your speed to the speed at which the limit point

Match your speed to the speed at which the limit point moves away from you providing you can stop within the distance that you can see to be clear.

appears to move. If it is moving away from you, accelerate. If it is coming closer to you or standing still, decelerate or brake. Even if the bend is not constant, you can still match your speed to the apparent movement of the limit point, because this will vary with the curvature of the bend.

Approaching the bend

- At first the limit point appears to remain at the same point in the road. Reduce your speed to be able to stop safely within the remaining distance.

- As you approach the bend take information about the sharpness of the bend and carefully assess the appropriate speed for cornering.

Going through the bend

- Just before you enter the bend the limit point begins to move round at a constant speed. Adjust your speed to the speed of this movement.

- You now have the correct speed for the bend. Select the gear to match this speed before entering the bend.

1

2

3

4

5

6

Coming out of the bend

- As the bend starts to straighten out your view begins to extend, and the limit point starts to move away more quickly. You then accelerate towards the limit point in proportion to the straightening out of your steering.
- As the bend comes to an end, continue to accelerate to catch the limit point until other considerations such as speed limits or new hazards restrict your acceleration.

These are the advantages of using the limit point together with the system:

- it ensures that you observe the driving safety rule of matching your speed to your ability to stop within the distance you can see to be clear
- it gives you the appropriate speed to approach and negotiate the bend
- it gives you the appropriate speed to go round the bend, and therefore the appropriate gear to be in
- it gives the point at which to start accelerating
- it is self-adjusting: as road visibility and conditions deteriorate you need more distance in which to stop, and so your speed must be reduced to compensate.

7

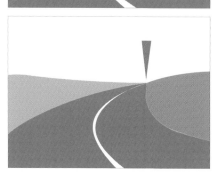

8

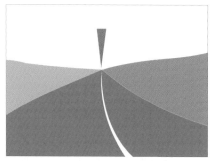

9

Using the system for cornering

This section takes you through the five phases of the system identifying key considerations at each phase and explaining how to use limit point analysis in the speed phase. As with any other use of the system, you should work through it methodically selecting the phases that are appropriate.

Information phase

On the approach to a corner or bend you should be constantly scanning the road for information, but specifically you need to look for:

- the traffic in front and behind
- the road surface and the effect of weather conditions on it
- the severity of the bend
- the limit point.

Seek out opportunities to look across the bend through gaps in hedges or between buildings. Look at the line of curvature of hedgerows and lamp posts to give you more information about the severity of the bend. Avoid becoming preoccupied with the bend – look for early warning of other hazards as well.

Position phase

You need to consider three things when deciding where to position your vehicle for cornering:

- safety
- information needs
- reducing the tightness of the bend.

Safety

Position yourself so that you are least likely to come into conflict with other road users, taking into account the length of your vehicle. On tight bends be aware of the need to allow for trailer cutting. Look out for pedestrians to your nearside and oncoming traffic to your offside. Safety is the overriding consideration. If you can safely adopt one of the positions suggested below do so, but never sacrifice safety for position.

Information needs

Your road position will determine how much you can see when you enter a bend. The position which gives you the greatest view depends on whether the bend is a left-hand bend or a right-hand bend. For a right bend the best viewing position is towards the nearside and for a left bend it is towards the offside. But always put safety first.

- **Right-hand bends** – position yourself towards the left of your road space. Be wary of parked vehicles and pedestrians and give them sufficient clearance. Other dangers to consider are blind junctions or exits, adverse cambers and poor condition of the nearside road surface.

For right-hand bends, the nearside gives an earlier view into the bend.

 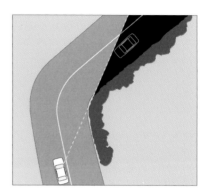

- **Left-hand bends** – position yourself towards the centre line so that you get an early view round the bend. Before you adopt this position consider:
- approaching traffic and other offside dangers which require a greater margin of safety
- whether your position might mislead other traffic as to your intentions
- whether any advantage would be gained at low speed or on an open bend.

For left-hand bends, a position towards the centre of the road gives an earlier view.

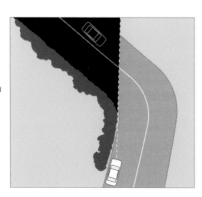 

Reducing the tightness of the bend

The other thing to consider is reducing the tightness of the curve through which you drive. By moving your vehicle from one side of the available road space to the other you can follow a shallower curve and thereby improve stability. The path you take is different for a right- or a left-hand bend, but always consider safety first. Do not take a straighter course unless you can see ahead clearly. Often you will not be able to do this until the road begins to straighten out.

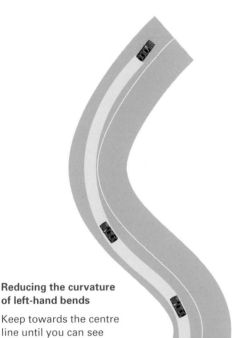

Reducing the curvature of right-hand bends

If you have a view across a bend and there is no oncoming traffic, take a gradually curving path towards the centre of the road. Then ease the vehicle back towards a more normal position on the other side of the bend. Under no circumstances must any other road users be endangered. Look at the diagram to the left and you can see that the curve made by the vehicle following this course is straighter than the curve of the bend itself.

Reducing the curvature of left-hand bends

Keep towards the centre line until you can see clearly ahead. Then drive your vehicle through a gradual curved path towards the nearside of the road, moving into a more normal position on the other side of the bend.

Speed phase

When you have adopted an appropriate position, the next phase of the system is to consider and obtain the appropriate speed to enter the bend.

Use the limit point to judge the safe speed to drive round the bend. Where the curve round the bend is constant, the limit point moves away from you at a constant speed. This gives you the speed for the bend unless the curvature changes. If the bend tightens, the limit point appears to move closer to you, and you should adjust your speed accordingly to remain within the safe stopping distance.

When assessing the speed to go round a bend, you need to consider:
• your vehicle's characteristics
• the road and road surface conditions
• the traffic conditions
• the weather conditions.

When you assess the situation, do not think, 'What is the fastest that I can go round this bend?' but rather, 'Can I stop in the distance I can see to be clear?' – that is, just before the limit point.

Gear phase

When you have achieved the right speed and before entering the bend, engage the appropriate gear for that speed. Select the gear that gives you greatest flexibility.

Think also about your expected acceleration on the far side of the bend. If you expect to come out of the bend into a 30mph area, then gentle acceleration would be appropriate. If the speed restriction on the other side of the bend is the national speed limit, consider entering the bend in a gear that will provide maximum acceleration out of it. The condition of the road surface needs to be included in these considerations: in wet or slippery conditions, harsh acceleration in a low gear may well result in wheel spin and a loss of steering control.

Acceleration phase

Depress the accelerator sufficiently to maintain a stable speed round the bend. Providing there are no additional hazards, start to accelerate when the limit point begins to move away and you begin to straighten your steering. (Check that no vehicles are attempting to overtake you first.)

As you continue to straighten your steering, increase your acceleration to 'catch' the limit point. Accelerate until you reach the speed limit or other speed limiting considerations.

Review

In this chapter we have looked at:

the four principles of safe cornering

the forces acting on a vehicle on bends and corners

the characteristics that affect a vehicle's ability to corner

how camber affects the ability to corner

the use of the system of vehicle control for cornering

the technique of limit point analysis

how to position yourself on the approach to a bend

how to reduce the curvature of a bend

how to assess the speed for a bend.

13 Overtaking

Developing your skill at overtaking safely

This chapter explains how to use the system of vehicle control to overtake and identifies the additional hazards that you need to consider to carry out the manoeuvre safely.

Overtaking is hazardous because it may bring you into the path of other vehicles. Applying the system of vehicle control enables you to carry out the manoeuvre safely.

Key safety points

When considering whether to overtake, always follow this safety advice:

- do not overtake where you cannot see far enough ahead to be sure it is safe
- avoid causing other vehicles (overtaken, following or approaching) to alter course or speed
- always be able to move back to the nearside in plenty of time
- always be ready to abandon overtaking if a new hazard comes into view
- do not overtake in situations where you might come into conflict with other road users (these are identified in the overtaking section of the *Highway Code*)
- avoid making a third line of moving vehicles wherever possible
- never overtake on the nearside on dual carriageways except in slow-moving queues of traffic when offside queues are moving more slowly.

Remember that overtaking is your decision and you can reconsider it at any point.

Overtaking stationary vehicles

Overtaking stationary vehicles is relatively straightforward. Use the system to approach and assess the hazard, and to pass it with safety. Take account of the position and speed of oncoming traffic, the position and speed of following traffic and the presence of pedestrians. If the situation allows, keep at least a door's width away from the side of the stationary vehicle.

Overtaking moving vehicles

Overtaking a moving vehicle is more complicated because the hazards are moving and the situation changes all the time. You need to consider the speed and acceleration capabilities of your own vehicle, and the relative speeds of other vehicles. You also need to be able to predict where vehicles and gaps in the traffic will converge. To do this safely requires careful observation and planning, good judgement of speed and distance, and an awareness of the many possible secondary hazards.

How to overtake

When you are catching up with another vehicle you should decide whether to adjust your speed and follow while it makes reasonable progress, or to overtake at the first safe opportunity. Whatever your decision, careful use of acceleration sense will assist the ease and smoothness of your manoeuvre. If you decide to overtake, assess whether you can approach and overtake in one continuous manoeuvre, or whether you will have to follow for a while until a suitable opportunity arises. Either way, the vehicle in front is a hazard so you need to consider the various phases of the system to deal with it safely.

You will meet other road users besides vehicles, and you need to consider their special needs. Avoid startling horses. Be aware that cyclists, especially children, can be erratic and allow them plenty of room. Give motorcycles good clearance and be aware that if you are too close your slip stream could destabilise them.

The following pages explain how to use the system of vehicle control to tackle the two overtaking situations we have identified:

- the absence of other hazards allows you to approach and overtake in one manoeuvre

- other hazards require you to take up a following position before you can overtake.

Overtaking in the absence of other hazards

You have identified that there is only one hazard present – the vehicle ahead that you are gaining on – and all the other conditions (such as clear view, sufficient space and absence of oncoming traffic) are suitable for immediate overtaking. Take the decision to overtake and work through the appropriate stages of the system to pass the slower vehicle(s) in one smooth manoeuvre.

Acceleration

Adjust your speed to return to the identified gap, and continue with your journey.

Gear

Select the most responsive gear for the speed.

Speed

Adjust your speed to complete the manoeuvre within the road space you know to be clear, and before any approaching vehicle could come into conflict with you.

Information

Observe the road ahead for road signs and markings, layout, approaching vehicles, other hazards, and any obstructed views which could conceal hazards. Identify a safe return gap. Observe the speed and position of any vehicles behind you. Judge the relative speeds of your own vehicle and the vehicle(s) to be overtaken. Plan your overtaking manoeuvre. Give a clear signal of your intention to overtake.

Position

At the appropriate point, take a course to overtake the vehicle ahead.

Overtaking when other hazards require you to take up a following position

This occurs when the presence of approaching vehicles, obscured views or some other hazard requires you to follow the vehicle(s) ahead before you can overtake safely. Overtaking in this situation requires a three-stage approach as illustrated on the right.

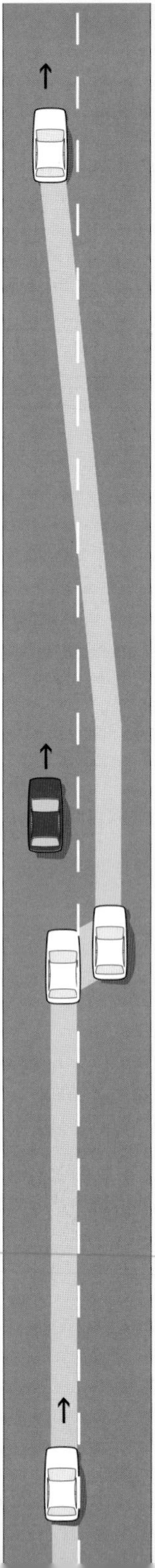

Stage 3
overtaking

Stage 2
the overtaking position

Stage 1
the following position

Stage one: the following position

Where you are gaining on a vehicle in front, and it is not possible to overtake immediately, use the system of vehicle control to reduce your speed to that of the vehicle in front to follow at a safe distance.

Your main task in the following position is to observe and assess the road and traffic conditions for an opportunity to overtake safely. You need to ask yourself the questions below.

Is it sensible to try to overtake the vehicle in front?

Are the drivers ahead likely to overtake?

Is there a possibility of as yet unseen vehicles approaching at high speed?

What is happening behind: are any of the drivers behind likely to overtake you?

What is the speed and length of the vehicle(s) to be overtaken?

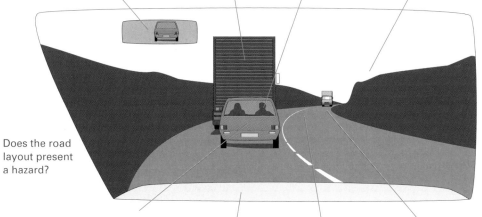

Does the road layout present a hazard?

What will be the likely response of the driver and occupants of the vehicle in front?

Have you taken into account the speed and performance of your own vehicle?

What is the distance needed to overtake and regain a nearside gap safely?

What is the speed of approaching vehicles in view?

Observe what is happening in the far distance, the middle ground, the immediate foreground and behind; do this repeatedly and look in the mirror frequently.

Your safety depends on making the correct interpretation of what you see. It is not enough just to see it.

In some circumstances it may be possible, as you close up on a vehicle in front, to miss out stage one and go straight to stage two: the overtaking position. This is determined by your view of the road ahead and whether any additional hazards are present that would make the overtaking position unsafe. If you do go straight to the overtaking position you still need to observe and assess the hazards identified in the diagram.

Stage two: the overtaking position

The overtaking position is closer than the following position and minimises the distance you have to travel to overtake. It can also indicate to the driver in front that you wish to overtake. Adopt this position so that you are ready to overtake when a safe opportunity arises.

Because it is closer than the following position you have less time to react to the actions of the vehicle in front, so you must be sure that there are no hazards ahead which might cause it to brake suddenly. You can only know this if you have been able to fully observe the road ahead.

Work through the stages of the system to move up to the overtaking position.

Information

Observe the road ahead, behind and to the side for an opportunity to safely occupy the overtaking position. Take into account hazards that can be seen and the possible dangers in areas that cannot be seen. Plan your move when you see an opportunity developing. Remember the need for rear observation if you do not know what is in your blind spot. Remember the *Highway Code* advice mirror – signal – manoeuvre.

Position

Move up to the overtaking position. This is the closest position to the vehicle in front that is consistent with the hazards and that gives an adequate view of the road ahead. It is not possible to define this position exactly: it depends on an awareness of the possible dangers, good judgement and experience.

Take views to the offside, nearside, through the windows and under and over the vehicle in front.

Avoid sitting in the blind spot of any vehicles you intend to overtake. Be aware that the closer you get to the vehicle in front the more likely you are to intimidate the driver.

The larger the vehicle in front, the further back you need to be.

With large vehicles and where it helps, take a view along both sides of the vehicle.

Speed

Adjust your speed to that of the vehicle in front.

Gear

If you are not already in an appropriate gear, select the most responsive gear for the speed, bearing in mind that this is the gear you will use to accelerate as you overtake. Do not choose too low a gear in an attempt to avoid braking when you return to the nearside after overtaking. Good observation, judgement and acceleration sense should enable you to return to the nearside without braking.

As the overtaking position is closer than the following position you must observe carefully for any new hazards. If a hazard comes into sight, consider dropping back to the following position until the hazard is passed. When planning to overtake you need to know exactly what is on the road ahead and to be aware of the possible pitfalls. Observation, planning, judgement of speed and distance and attention to detail are crucial. Thoughtless overtaking is dangerous.

Stage three: overtaking

From the overtaking position continue observing until you identify an opportunity to overtake, then re-run the system of vehicle control to guide you while overtaking.

Information

Identify:

- a safe stretch of road along which you have adequate vision

- a gap into which you can safely return

- the speed of any approaching vehicles

- the relative speed of your own vehicle and the vehicle(s) you intend to overtake

- what is happening behind – give any necessary signals

- any road or landscape features that could conceal a rapidly approaching vehicle.

Remember the *Highway Code* advice mirror – signal – manoeuvre. Consider the benefits of giving a headlight or horn signal.

Position

Having made a thorough information check and decided it is safe to go, re-check your mirrors, give appropriate signals and move out to an offside position. Generally, do this without accelerating. From this new position make a thorough information check of the road ahead and behind for any unidentified hazards. Decide whether to continue with overtaking.

Speed

Overtake if the situation is clear, adjusting your speed if necessary. While you are in the offside position you are in a zone of potential danger so move through it as briskly as possible.

Gear

Before overtaking you should have selected a suitable gear. Sometimes circumstances may require another gear change, but you should generally avoid this during the overtaking manoeuvre.

Acceleration

Adjust your speed to complete the overtaking manoeuvre safely, and to enter the gap you have identified. Where possible, use acceleration sense to adjust your speed, but use the brakes if necessary.

If you are overtaking in a line of traffic and the offside position provides a good view, consider the opportunity for further overtaking before you return to the nearside position. If you have considered all aspects of the system and it is safe to proceed, take the opportunity and move on to the new safe gap that you have identified.

Summary

The diagram below summarises the overtaking manoeuvre described in stage three:

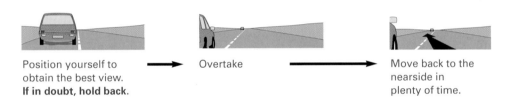

Position yourself to obtain the best view. **If in doubt, hold back.**   Overtake   Move back to the nearside in plenty of time.

Remember the *Highway Code* advice: mirrors – signal – manoeuvre.

Special hazards to consider before attempting to overtake

In the first part of this chapter we have worked through two methods for overtaking systematically. To present these as clearly as possible we have not introduced other aspects of road and traffic conditions which must be considered before overtaking. These considerations are essential to safety, and are explored next.

The *Highway Code* has a section which gives advice on overtaking. The illustrations on the following page show some common collision situations that can arise if this advice is not followed.

  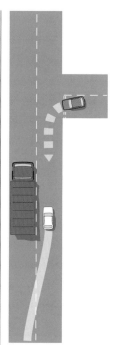 

The driver of the white car does not realise that the driver of the blue car can see only the slow-moving bus and may move out into the path of the white car. This is a common cause of collisions when filtering.

The driver of the white car fails to foresee that the red car may turn without warning into a side road, cutting across the path of the overtaking car.

The driver of the white car fails to appreciate that the driver of the green car is looking only to his right and may pull out as the overtaking car approaches on the wrong side of the road.

The driver of the white car fails to appreciate that the lorry is not indicating to overtake the car ahead, but is turning right.

The range of hazards you must consider

Before overtaking you must consider the full range of possible hazards that each situation presents:

- the vehicle in front

- the vehicle behind

- the road layout and conditions

- road surface

- overtaking in a stream of vehicles
- overtaking on a single carriageway
- right-hand bends
- left-hand bends
- overtaking on a dual carriageway.

Each of these is discussed below.

The vehicle in front

Assess what sort of hazard the vehicle in front presents.

- Has the driver of the vehicle noticed you?
- Can you predict from earlier behaviour whether the response of the driver is likely to be aggressive?
- Does the size or the load of the vehicle prevent the driver from seeing you or prevent you from seeing the road ahead clearly?

Make your intention to overtake clear to the driver in front. Your road position and following distance help you to do this, but take care not to appear too intimidating. This can be counter-productive and provoke an aggressive response in the other driver who might speed up as you try to overtake. If the driver in front appears to be obstructive, consider the implications. First, is it worthwhile overtaking at all and second, how much extra speed and space do you need to allow for this?

If the driver in front has not noticed your presence or has a load which obscures the rear view mirrors, take this into account. Consider the use of the headlights or horn to inform the driver of your presence.

Take extra care before overtaking a long vehicle. If appropriate, take views to both sides of the vehicle and ensure that there is ample space to overtake and return safely to your own side. The same applies to vehicles that have wide or high loads: be sure that you have observed carefully and are aware of any possible dangers in the road ahead.

The vehicle behind

Assess whether the vehicles behind pose a risk. Note their speed, position and progress, and judge whether they may attempt to overtake you. Be aware that other vehicles may come forward from behind the vehicle behind you. Remember to give clear signals that accurately convey your intentions. Use your mirrors to monitor the situation behind you, especially before changing your speed or position.

Road layout and conditions

When planning to overtake, consider the layout of the road ahead very carefully. Look for nearside obstructions or junctions (including pathways, tracks, entrances, farm gates) out of which vehicles or other hazards could emerge and cause the vehicle(s) you intend to overtake suddenly to veer to the offside. On the offside, look carefully for junctions, especially where they could conceal emerging vehicles or other hazards.

Look for lay-bys on both sides of the road and be alert to the possibility that a vehicle might pull out of them. Be especially attentive to offside lay-bys. Drivers leaving them may not see you because they are concentrating on what is happening behind rather than in front of them.

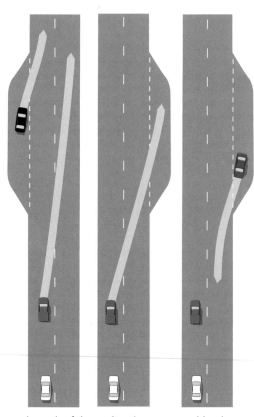

Bends, hill crests, hump back bridges and any other aspect of road layout which could obscure your view must be taken into account. Allow for the possibility that there are fast-moving vehicles approaching you on the sections of road you cannot see. Follow the basic rules for overtaking:

- identify a gap into which you can return and the point along the road at which you will be able to enter it

- judge whether you will be able to reach that point before any approaching vehicle, seen or unseen, could come into conflict with you.

In each of these situations approaching lay-bys, the white car should be wary of overtaking. The arrows show the possible actions of traffic ahead.

You should have observed the whole stretch of road necessary to complete the manoeuvre, and know that it does not include any other hazards. Look especially for hazards which might cause the vehicles you are overtaking to alter their position. Make full use of road signs and road markings, especially those giving instructions or warning you of hazards ahead.

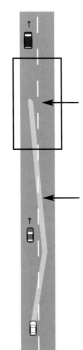

The basic rule for overtaking

If this is the gap you have identified as the one into which you will return...

...then this is the earliest point at which you can start to enter that gap.

Can you reach this point before any approaching vehicles – seen or unseen – could come into conflict with you?

Road surface

The condition of the road surface should always be taken into account before you overtake. There may be ruts or holes which could throw a vehicle off course, or surface water which could cause a curtain of spray at a critical moment. The effects of adverse weather on road holding and visibility must always be taken into account.

Overtaking in a stream of vehicles

Overtaking in a stream of vehicles is more difficult because it takes more time. You also have to take into account the possible actions of more drivers both in front and behind. There is always the possibility that drivers in front are not aware of your presence or intention to overtake and that drivers behind might attempt to overtake you.

Before overtaking, you should identify a clear gap between the vehicles in front which you can enter safely. Be aware that the gap may close up before you arrive, so choose gaps that are large enough to allow for this. Do not overtake if you will have to force your vehicle into a gap.

Where a queue has formed because of an obstruction in the road ahead, do not attempt to jump the queue. This invariably annoys other road users and can be dangerous.

Overtaking on a single carriageway

Overtaking on a single carriageway is perhaps the most hazardous form of overtaking. While you are overtaking, your vehicle is in the path of any oncoming vehicles so great care must be taken before deciding on the manoeuvre.

Develop the ability to judge the speed and distance of oncoming vehicles accurately. You need to be able to assess whether you can reach the return gap before they do. Remember you always have the option of deciding not to overtake. Judging the speed of an oncoming vehicle is extremely difficult, especially on long straight roads. The size and type of the approaching vehicle may give you an indication of its possible speed.

Plan and prepare your overtaking carefully. As well as looking for vehicles, train yourself to look specifically for motorcyclists, cyclists and pedestrians before you overtake. If you do not expect to see something, you may not see it when it is there – an oncoming pedestrian or cyclist can be easily overlooked.

Overtaking on right-hand bends

 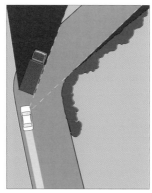 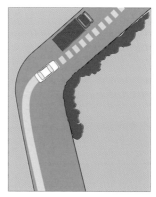

Where the vehicle in front is approaching the apex of a right-hand bend with a restricted view, you should select a course well to the nearside.

Move up on the vehicle in front just before it reaches the apex so that you gain the earliest possible view along its offside.

Overtake if the road is clear, as long as there is no risk of losing tyre adhesion and you have adequate nearside clearance during the manoeuvre. If conditions are not favourable for overtaking, drop back.

Overtaking on left-hand bends

 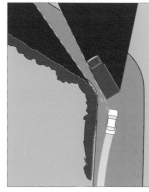 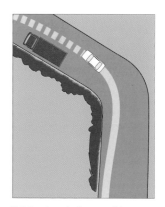

Where the leading vehicle approaches a blind left bend do not attempt to overtake until you have a clear view of the road ahead.

You could maintain a position where you can see along the nearside of the leading vehicle as it passes through the bend.

If this view is favourable move out to look along the offside as the road straightens and start to overtake when conditions are suitable. Bear in mind that areas of the road will be obscured while you change from a nearside to an offside view, so take great care when you do this.

█████ obstructed vision

Single carriageway roads marked with three lanes

Single carriageway roads marked with three lanes are potentially
very dangerous as the overtaking lane in each direction is the
shared centre lane. Never attempt to overtake on such a road if
there is the possibility of an approaching vehicle moving into the
centre lane. Avoid overtaking when you would make a third line of
moving vehicles unless you are sure it is absolutely safe to do so.

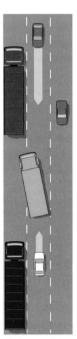

Avoid the temptation
to follow another
vehicle through an
apparently safe gap
on a three-lane single
carriageway. Always
assess a safe return
position for yourself.
The leading vehicle
may well be able to
slip safely into place
on the nearside
leaving you stranded
in the middle faced
by oncoming
vehicles.

When you are judging
speed and distance to
overtake and a vehicle
is approaching, look
out for the presence of
the 'lurker'. This is a
vehicle which closes
right up behind other
vehicles and then
sweeps out into full
view. Do not assume
that the drivers of light
vehicles or cars behind
a heavy lorry are
content to stay where
they are. They could
well pull out just when
you are overtaking.

Overtaking on dual carriageways

On dual carriageways it can be more difficult to judge the speed of
traffic approaching from the rear.

Before overtaking watch carefully the vehicles in the nearside lanes.
If one of them is closing up on the vehicle in front, the driver may
pull out, possibly without signalling or only signalling as the vehicle
starts to move out. A good guide is the distance between the
wheels of the vehicle and the lane markings. If the gap narrows, the
vehicle could be moving out. Overtaking when it would cause three
vehicles to be abreast should be avoided if possible, although on

many motorways this is difficult. You should always overtake on the right on dual carriageways except when traffic is moving in queues and the queue on the right is moving more slowly than you are.

Assisting others to overtake

Assisting others to overtake eases tensions and improves the quality of driving for everyone on the road. The key element is your attitude of mind when you drive. You should not regard driving as a competition but as a means of travelling between two points as safely as possible. Try to regard your driving dispassionately and keep an eye on yourself to identify any inappropriate responses. If other drivers wish to overtake you, assist them:

• be alert to the intentions of drivers behind you: use your mirrors and assess whether they wish to overtake or not

• allow enough distance between you and the vehicle in front for the overtaking vehicle to enter the gap.

Be aware of the likely dangers on the approach and exit from areas where the speed limit is lower than the national speed limit. Other drivers are quite likely to attempt to overtake you while you observe the legal speed limit. This is likely to happen:

• when you slow down to enter a lower speed limit area

• when you are about to leave a lower speed limit area.

Review

In this chapter we have looked at:

how to overtake safely

how to overtake in the absence of other hazards

the three-stage approach to overtaking when other hazards cause you to take up a following position

the hazards that you should consider before overtaking

14 Motorway driving

Developing your skill at motorway driving

Although this chapter is called motorway driving much of it is applicable to driving on dual carriageways. The speed limit for cars is the same on many dual carriageways as it is on motorways, but the absence of a hard shoulder and the presence of lay-bys and crossroads make dual carriageways especially hazardous.

Before you join the motorway

The *Highway Code*

The *Highway Code* contains advice on motorway driving, and includes information on motorway signs and regulations. You should know these sections thoroughly. This chapter discusses the techniques which will help you to implement the *Highway Code* advice more effectively.

Special features of motorways

You need to prepare adequately before you join a motorway. These are the special conditions you should consider:

- the speed and volume of the traffic
- the limited occurrence of refreshment and refuelling areas
- the dangers of stopping on the hard shoulder
- the level of attention required
- the legal limitations on certain vehicles using the motorway.

Each of these affects your safety. High speeds mean that hazardous situations develop quickly and that you travel further before you can react. Minimum stopping distances are greatly extended and collisions often cause serious injury and damage. As the volume of traffic increases, the demands on your attention and decision-making also increase. With more vehicles there are more hazards and the opportunities for manoeuvre are more restricted.

Joining the motorway

Which lane is which?

This chapter uses the numbering system used by the police and other emergency services to refer to motorway lanes.

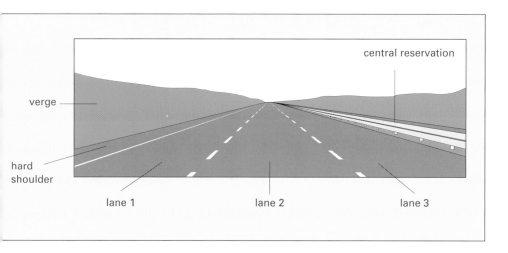

verge

hard shoulder

central reservation

lane 1   lane 2   lane 3

The nearside lane is lane 1, and the other lanes are numbered in sequence to the furthest offside lane. On a three-lane motorway lane 1 is the lane next to the hard shoulder and lane 3 is the lane next to the central reservation. The hard shoulder is not counted as a carriageway lane.

Joining the motorway at a slip road or where motorways merge is hazardous and you should use the system of vehicle control to approach and join. Slip roads are designed to give drivers the time and space to merge smoothly with traffic on the main carriageway. They are often elevated and you should take advantage of the high viewpoint to observe the traffic flow and to plan your approach. Skilful use of the system should enable you to join the motorway without causing other drivers to alter course or speed. Drivers on the motorway have priority and may not be able to move over to allow you to enter, but with early vision, planning and acceleration sense you should be able to merge safely. Only poor planning or exceptionally heavy traffic will cause you to stop in the acceleration lane.

Slip roads have one or more lanes. If you are travelling in an offside lane of the slip road, consider how your speed and position will affect the access of nearside vehicles on to the motorway. If you overtake a vehicle to your nearside just before joining the motorway you could block its path. You are in danger of colliding with it if you cannot move straight into lane 2 of the motorway.

Do not overtake a vehicle travelling in the inside lane of the slip road if this would block the entry of that vehicle on to the motorway.

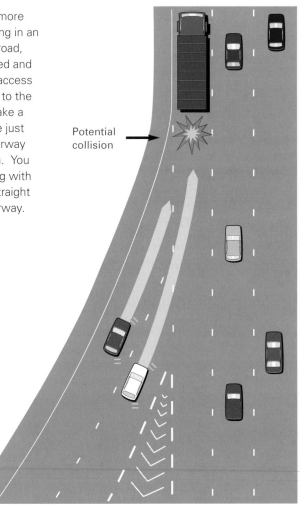

Potential collision

Use the system

As you enter the motorway all five phases of the system are relevant. You need to take sufficient information about the traffic on the slip road and motorway to ensure that you are in the right position, at the right speed, in the right gear to accelerate on to the motorway smoothly and in safety.

Signalling

As you are about to enter lane 1 of the motorway give a clear signal to inform motorists already on the motorway of your intention to join the traffic flow.

Before you join the motorway check over your shoulder to make sure there is nothing in your blind spot.

Acceleration

As the speeds on motorways are higher than on the rest of the road system, you should allow yourself time to adjust to driving at speed and to the speeds of other vehicles.

Observation

Because of the speeds involved, extended observation on the motorway is essential:

- look ahead and behind you right up to the road horizons
- scan ahead, to the sides and to the rear frequently and thoroughly
- use your mirrors regularly – you should know at all times what is happening behind you
- be aware of the blind spots on your vehicle and those of other drivers and be prepared to move your body and alter vehicle position to observe what is happening in those areas
- monitor what is happening to your vehicle – regularly check that the instruments are giving normal readings, listen to the sound of your engine and to the noise of the tyres on the road surface
- check your speed regularly on the speedometer – it is very easy to increase speed without realising it
- be especially alert around junctions – traffic patterns change rapidly in these areas.

Adapting to higher speeds

At 70mph you travel 31 metres per second (over 100 ft per second). At such speeds you need as much time to react as possible:

- extend your observations in all directions and to the road horizons to give yourself more time

- anticipate early and maintain a safe following distance – in good weather the two-second rule provides a good guide but in poor weather conditions this distance needs to be greatly extended

- avoid coarse steering at speed

- give other drivers sufficient time to see your signals before making a manoeuvre

- wind and engine noise can drown the sound of your horn at high speeds, so consider using your headlights as an effective alternative.

Lane discipline

Good lane discipline is essential for motorway driving. There are no slow or fast lanes. Overtake only to the right, except when traffic is moving in queues and the queue on your right is moving more slowly than you are. Remember your mirror checks before changing lanes in either direction

Overtaking

Before overtaking be alert for:

- slower vehicles moving out in front of you

- faster vehicles coming up behind you.

Apply the system of vehicle control to overtake safely on motorways and pay special attention to the information phase.

Taking information

The high speeds of motorway traffic make it necessary to take information carefully before making any manoeuvre. Scan regularly so that you are continually aware of the pattern of surrounding traffic. You should know which vehicles are closing up on other vehicles in front, and which vehicles are moving up behind. Constantly monitor opportunities to overtake and match your speed of approach to coincide with an opportunity. Make allowances for the additional hazards presented by lane closures and motorway junctions.

Look for early warnings of the intention of other drivers to overtake. Indications of another driver's intention to move out are:

- relative speeds

- head movements

- body movements

- vehicle movement from the centre of the lane towards the white lane markers.

You are likely to see all these before the driver signals: many drivers only signal as they start to change lanes.

Overtaking on left-hand bends when lanes 1 and 2 are mainly occupied by heavy goods or large vehicles needs to be considered carefully. There is always the possibility that a car is hidden between the heavy goods vehicles and is about to pull out into lane 3. In these circumstances make sure you can stop in the distance you can see to be clear. Do not attempt to overtake unless you are sure you can see all the vehicles in lane 2 and well into the gaps between them so you can be sure no small vehicles are concealed.

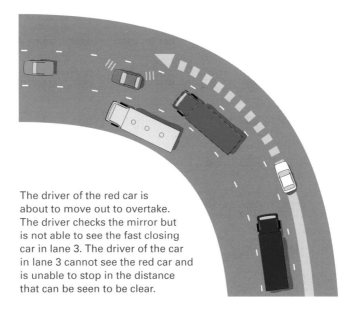

The driver of the red car is about to move out to overtake. The driver checks the mirror but is not able to see the fast closing car in lane 3. The driver of the car in lane 3 cannot see the red car and is unable to stop in the distance that can be seen to be clear.

Just before you overtake make a thorough check of the position and speed of the vehicles behind. Move your head to reduce the extent of the blind spot. Re-check the position and speed of vehicles to the front and then consider the information that you need to give to the surrounding traffic.

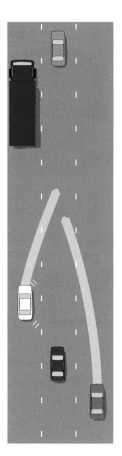

As you move from lane 1 to lane 2, beware of vehicles moving up behind you into lane 2 from lane 3.

Indicator signals

Give a clear indicator signal before changing lanes. Let the indicator flash long enough for other drivers to see and react to it.

When you have passed the vehicle or vehicles in front, return to the appropriate lane when a suitable opportunity arises but avoid excessive weaving.

Overtaking situations to avoid

You should generally avoid overtaking when to do so would create a line of three vehicles travelling abreast. In current traffic conditions this is often not possible but you should avoid situations like the one illustrated opposite (top) which leave you no room for manoeuvre.

This illustrates a problem for vehicles moving at speed and overtaking three abreast. The overtaking driver in the white car has no room for manoeuvre if a hazard arises. Movement into lane 1 or 2 is blocked by the vehicles in those lanes and escape through lane 3 is blocked by the vehicle ahead. Hold back until the vehicle in lane 3 has moved ahead of the vehicles in lane 2. This then gives you the option of an alternative position. Keep a watchful eye on your mirrors for vehicles closing up fast behind you.

Being overtaken

Anticipate the movement of vehicles behind you by their lane position and their speed of approach. By observing minor details in the way the traffic is behaving you will be forewarned before any signals or manoeuvres are made. This will help you to avoid potentially dangerous situations. Be aware that, as you are overtaken, you temporarily enter a blind spot for the overtaking driver.

Motorway junctions

At junctions and service areas, there are likely to be variations in the speed of the traffic flow and an increase in the number of vehicles changing lanes. Watch for drivers who delay changing lanes for an exit to the last second. When you see a motorway exit, anticipate the possibility of an entry slip road ahead and traffic joining the motorway.

If you are on the main carriageway, check your mirrors early and if possible allow traffic to join the motorway by making slight adjustments to your speed or changing to a lane on your right. However, do not move to a lane on your right if it forces existing motorway users to change their speed or position. Ultimately it is the vehicle joining the motorway that should give way, but be prepared in case it does not.

Watch for drivers who delay changing lanes for an exit road to the last second, and watch for traffic joining the motorway by slip roads ahead.

Leaving the motorway

Leaving the motorway should be carefully planned. Know well in advance at which junction you intend to leave. Assess the road and traffic conditions as you approach it and make use of the information provided by road signs and markings.

Exit information

The diagram below illustrates the exit information given at most motorway exits.

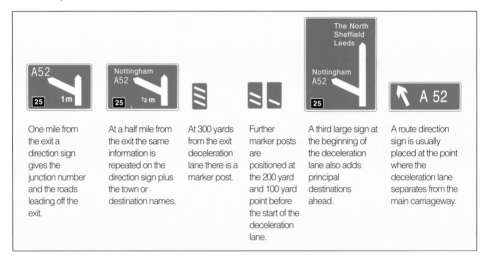

One mile from the exit a direction sign gives the junction number and the roads leading off the exit.	At a half mile from the exit the same information is repeated on the direction sign plus the town or destination names.	At 300 yards from the exit deceleration lane there is a marker post.	Further marker posts are positioned at the 200 yard and 100 yard point before the start of the deceleration lane.	A third large sign at the beginning of the deceleration lane also adds principal destinations ahead.	A route direction sign is usually placed at the point where the deceleration lane separates from the main carriageway.

As you approach your intended exit junction look for the advance direction boards and use the system of vehicle control to plan and carry out your exit. If the motorway is busy, consider joining the left-hand lane earlier rather than later. Always allow sufficient time for other drivers to react to your signals. Generally you should indicate no later than the 300 yard marker and if it would benefit other drivers you should indicate well before.

Avoid braking on the main carriageway if possible and plan to lose any unwanted road speed in the deceleration lane. On busy motorways be alert for vehicles attempting to leave the motorway late from the second or third lane and cutting across your path. Remember that high speeds will affect your perception of speed when you leave the motorway:

• check your speedometer regularly to help you adjust to the slower speeds of the ordinary road system

- plan for the point at which you will meet two-way traffic
- be alert for acute bends at the end of exit slip roads and watch for oil and tyre dust deposits which make these areas exceptionally slippery.

Lane closures

Roadworks are regularly encountered on motorway journeys. Contraflow systems are not dangerous in themselves but become dangerous when drivers fail to respond to advance warnings. All roadworks are signed on approach and the sequence of the signs is always the same and should be known. You should conform to the mandatory speed limits that often accompany roadworks, even when conditions seem to be suitable for a higher speed.

Merging with other traffic requires judgement and courtesy. A sensible policy is for vehicles from each lane to merge alternately. These situations have great potential for unnecessary conflict and therefore unnecessary collisions. Allow adequate following gaps, and do not close up tightly to prevent other vehicles merging. Drivers in the closed lane should avoid causing provocation by overtaking long queues of traffic waiting in the open lanes.

Matrix signs and signals are used on motorways to warn of lane closures or other changes in driving conditions ahead. You may not immediately be able to see the need to slow down or change lanes. Do not be complacent and assume the sign is a mistake. The incident it refers to may be some distance along the motorway.

Matrix signs warn of hazards that may be some distance ahead.

15 When things go wrong

We all hope that a collision is something we can avoid whilst driving. However, the fact of the matter is that we all need to know what our obligations are and how we should deal with the unexpected. Collisions, by definition, occur when we least expect them; on occasions we may be to blame and at other times we are the innocent party.

Whether we are to blame or not, it is important that we remain calm and avoid the mistake of apportioning blame. If you are ever involved in a collision, it is important that you make an accurate assessment of the situation; in all cases you must stop at the scene.

The severity of collision will dictate the way in which you should respond. If any person has suffered injury due to the occurrence, you are required by law to report the collision to the police as soon as possible and always within 24 hours. The only exception to this is if you have provided the injured party with the details of your insurance policy, vehicle registration number, full name and address along with the full name and address of the owner of the vehicle if appropriate. Should you be unable to supply all of this information in person to the other parties involved, you must inform the police of the collision as described above. Remember that if you collide with certain animals, you must report the incident; specified animals are horse, cattle, ass, mule, pig, sheep, goat or dog.

When you initially make an assessment of the scene of a road collision, there are many factors to consider. If there are goods vehicles involved, look to see if there are any Hazchem symbols displayed (like the one shown here).

If the collision involves a vehicle that is carrying hazardous chemicals, move everyone as far away from the vehicles involved as possible. Remember, when calling for the emergency services, to tell the operator that this is a Hazchem incident.

Check for fallen power lines, cables or leaking fuel. Remember that more and more cars are powered by LPG gas; if such a vehicle is involved in a road collision, clear the area as quickly as possible.

Initial actions at a collision scene

Below you will see two paths of action that should be taken initially at the scene of a collision.

Non-injury collision	Injury collision or carriageway obstructed
Ensure that everyone is clear of the road and well away from any potential danger.	Dial 999 and request the attendance of the emergency services.
All drivers involved in the collision should exchange their personal details – full names, addresses, contact telephone numbers and insurance details if to hand. Make sure that you record the registration numbers, makes and model of each vehicle involved.	Nominate uninjured people to warn approaching vehicles of the danger ahead, and assist with traffic control. Impose a smoking ban and ensure that mobile phones are not used at the scene. Check that all vehicle ignitions are turned off and handbrakes are applied.
Obtain the names and addresses of any witnesses to the collision.	Do not attempt to move any injured persons from a vehicle or the carriageway. The only exception to this would be if their lives were in immediate danger, such as in the case of a burning vehicle.
If you have any suspicion that one of the drivers has been drinking or has left the scene, call the police.	Never give an injured person anything to eat or drink. If an injured person is bleeding heavily, apply direct pressure to the wound using a clean piece of linen; this should stem profuse bleeding. If the wound is on an arm or leg, try to elevate the limb if at all possible. Re-assure the injured by informing them that assistance is *en route*.
	Once the emergency services arrive at the scene, remain there until you are told you can leave.

Once the primary safety tasks have been completed, it is a good thing to write down as much detail as possible regarding the circumstances of the collision. Include as many of the items from the tables below as you can.

Driver details

Name	
Address	
Telephone	
Insurer's name and address	
Insurance policy number	

Vehicle details

Registration number	
Make and model	
Colour	
General condition	
Apparent damage sustained	
Obvious defects, such as lights, tyres, etc.	

Vehicle activity

Describe vehicle's manoeuvres immediately prior to collision	
Was the vehicle in the correct lane and giving the correct signals?	
Was the vehicle towing a trailer of any description?	
Were the vehicle lights on or off?	

Date and location

Date and time of collision

Road name or number

Description of exact location

Speed limit

Conditions at the scene

Raining/snow/ice/fog/other
Road surface defects
Street lighting on/off/none
Road surface wet/dry/icy/ contaminated, e.g., oil

Injured parties

Names and addresses

Telephone(s)
Driver or passenger in which vehicle?
Record registration number
Pedestrian/cyclist/horse rider, etc.
Seat-belts worn (if applicable)?
Apparent injuries

Witnesses

Names and addresses

Telephone(s)

Location at time of collision

Observations/comments about the incident

Other property

Description of property damaged (include road signs, lamp posts, etc.)

Owner of damaged property

Police attendance

Name and collar number of police officer attending the scene

Officer's station and contact telephone number

If the collision is not reported at the scene, record name of police station that collision was reported at, along with date and time, and officer taking the report

Collision plan

Use the area below to make a sketch of the collision scene; include on your plan all road markings, the positions in which the vehicles came to rest, position of debris, skid marks and any damaged property. Try to locate a permanent fixed point at the scene and pace out the positions of the vehicles from that point – use something like a telegraph pole, road sign, drain cover, telephone kiosk or a similar object as a fixed point. Most telegraph posts, lighting poles and street signs have a reference number; it will be useful to make a note of any such identification. Mark on the plan approximately where each witness was at the time of the collision, this will help identify the witnesses that had the best view of the incident. If you have access to a camera then take pictures of the scene from various angles and take close up shots of the damage caused to the vehicles.

By completing all the items listed on the previous pages, you will have all the information needed to help the insurance companies and police (where appropriate) resolve the matter as quickly as possible.

Whilst at the scene of a collision remain calm, be courteous and give as much assistance to those who are in need of help as you possibly can.

Police involvement at a collision

If the police are called to the scene of a collision, do not panic. The police are there primarily to ensure that any risk to other road users encountering the collision scene may be minimised, to assist injured people and to generally co-ordinate the recovery of damaged vehicles. Obviously, the police will assess the collision scene. If it appears that one or more of the drivers may have committed road traffic offences that directly led to the collision, they are required to investigate further.

The investigation of a road collision usually involves taking statements from witnesses and interviewing drivers. If you are asked to make a statement then it usually indicates that you are not under suspicion of an offence at that time. A statement is your account of what occurred and the police officer will write down what you say. Making a statement is voluntary; most people have little reservation in making a statement as it is usually considered the best way of adding your perspective to an investigation.

Should you be requested to give an interview, then you are under a degree of suspicion of having committed an offence. Before an officer is able to interview a suspect, the officer has to plainly tell the interviewee of the availability of free independent legal advice and administer the caution prior to answering any questions. There are few occasions when it would be considered sensible to decline this offer. Having a legal representative will give you a sense of security in knowing that procedures are conducted correctly. It will also provide you with someone who can explain anything that you don't understand. By acting on years of training and general experience, your legal representative will be able to consider the evidence and help advise you on the courses of action available to you. During interview you have the right to remain silent, however on some occasions this may be counter productive. Discuss such options with your legal representative or solicitor.

There are a small number of serious road traffic offences for which a driver may be arrested. These are generally:

- driving whilst disqualified,

- driving whilst under the influence of alcohol or drugs,

- causing death by dangerous driving.

The most common of all these offences is driving whilst under the influence of alcohol. As a professional driver you know the value of your licence, so the next time you are tempted to have 'one for the road', make it a Coke!

If following a collision you are arrested, you will be conveyed to the nearest designated police station where the reason for your arrest will be outlined to the custody officer. If your arrest is authorised then you will be informed of your rights – to have someone else informed of your arrest, to consult a copy of the codes of practice covering police powers and procedures and the right to free independent legal advice. As stated previously it is good advice to consult with a legal representative at the earliest practical opportunity.

If you have been arrested for a drink–drive offence, the station procedures will not be delayed whilst a solicitor travels to the station. If you fail to comply with the requests made to provide samples, you will be charged with failing to provide a sample. This offence carries an automatic disqualification following conviction.

As an authorised detainee at a police station, you may be kept in custody for up to 24 hours. In special circumstances this could be extended to 72 hours. The majority of detainees are released well before the 24-hour deadline. If you have been arrested for a drink–drive offence, in certain circumstances you will be kept in custody until the next available court. If this is the case and you are found guilty, your driving disqualification will start immediately.

Fixed penalty notices

There are two types of fixed penalty notices which may be issued within the UK. These are referred to as non-endorsable and endorsable.

Endorsable notices mean that they carry penalty points (maximum of three) and a fine which is currently set at £60. Non-endorsable notices carry no penalty points, however there is a fixed £30 fine. If issued with a fixed penalty notice, you must ensure that the fine is paid within 28 days of the offence. If you have been asked to produce any driving documents these must be presented at a police station within seven days, failure to comply with any aspects of the scheme will result in a court summons.

A fixed penalty is always the minimum penalty for any given offence. Every person issued with a fixed penalty notice within the UK has a right to request a court hearing, however, should you elect to go to court and are subsequently found to be guilty, you will have to pay at least the minimum fine plus any court costs awarded against you. If you do intend contesting a fixed penalty notice, it is worth consulting a solicitor first.

Speeding offences

This is probably the most common issue that leads to a police officer making an acquaintance with an otherwise law-abiding citizen. Many drivers have experienced the cold sweat and thumping heart rate that seems to grip them the moment the blue lights are turned on!

Speed checks are a fact of life and if you really want to avoid that sinking feeling in the pit of your stomach, the embarrassment and inconvenience of being pulled over and having your licence endorsed, you really must pay particular attention to speed limits.

If you are stopped for speeding, then generally you will be offered a fixed penalty ticket. This is the cheapest and most convenient way of dealing with the matter. You will have 28 days in which to pay a £60 fine directly to the court office, and seven days to produce your insurance policy, M.O.T. certificate (if appropriate) and surrender your driving licence at a police station of your choice. As long as you comply with these conditions your licence will be endorsed with three penalty points and you will avoid a trip to the local magistrates court (local to the scene of the offence).

Police officers use sophisticated measuring devices such as Vascar units and laser guns to calculate a vehicle's speed. All speed measuring devices used by the police are approved by the Home Office and as such, magistrates will place a great deal of faith in the results recorded when used by a trained operator. It is very rare for speeding cases to be successfully defended. It is for this reason that most solicitors will advise clients to accept a fixed penalty notice rather than appear in court.

If you have exceeded the speed limit by a considerable margin, you are likely to be summonsed to attend court. Similarly if you have over eight penalty points on your licence at the time you are stopped, the police officer will not be able to issue a fixed penalty notice. In these circumstances you will be summonsed to court. If this happens to you, then you should consult a solicitor regarding the incident. Motorists who appear in court for speeding offences are there for the magistrates to consider whether a term of disqualification should be imposed. As a person who relies on a driving licence to carry out your daily work this could have serious implications. Ensure that you are properly represented at court. It could be the difference between retaining your licence or losing your job.

Review

In this chapter we have looked at:

Which types of collision need to be reported to the police

What documents you should produce

What details you need to take note of at the scene

How to deal with a fixed penalty notice

	Built-up areas	Single carriageways	Dual carriageways	Motorways
Cars and motorcycles (including car, derived vans up to 2 tonnes maximum laden weight)	30	60	70	70
Cars towing caravans or trailers (including car, derived vans and motorcycles)	30	50	60	60
Buses or coaches (not exceeding 12 metres in overall length)	30	50	60	70
Goods vehicles (not exceeding 7.5 tonnes maximum laden weight)	30	50	60	70
Goods vehicles (exceeding 7.5 tonnes maximum laden weight)	30	40	50	60

16 Tachographs

A basic understanding of tachographs is valuable to anyone who drives a vehicle for an employer. This chapter should be viewed as a basic introduction to driver's hours and tachographs, primarily aimed at drivers of smaller goods vehicles up to 7.5 tonnes, which are used for duties which would bring the driver back to the usual operating base on most days. The rules outlined in this chapter are EC driver's hours rules, the most commonly used rules for drivers within the UK driving vehicles fitted with tachographs. This chapter does not cover the rules associated with international travel, double manned vehicles or passenger carrying vehicles (PCV). All drivers who have a responsibility to comply with tachograph legislation should endeavour to gain as much knowledge of the subject as possible, as with all law – ignorance is not a defence. The penalties for committing driver's hours offences are considerable with fines up to £5000 and many tachograph deception offences carry custodial punishment.

You may never have driven a vehicle fitted with a tachograph. However, what if you were asked tomorrow to cover for a colleague who has been taken ill? You always like to help any way you can and you happily agree. So when you jump into the driving seat of your mate's twin axle long wheelbase van and see a rather bulky looking speedometer staring back at you, what do you do? Ignore it – I don't need to bother with that, I'm only covering for the one day? Have a fiddle and try and fit one of those paper discs inside and hope for the best? Or spend a while finding out what it's all about and how it works?

If you take the responsible option and spend a little while reading through the next chapter, it may well save you and your transport manager a whole load of grief. Here you will find in simple terms when a tachograph unit needs to be installed and used, and what your responsibilities are as the driver.

Which vehicles need Tachograph units fitted

In relation to tachographs, goods vehicles with a maximum gross train weight exceeding 3.5 tonnes, and which are used for the commercial carriage of goods, are required to have a tachograph fitted. If driving a vehicle that is not considered a goods vehicle, but you attach a trailer for the carriage of goods, then this vehicle will be governed by tachograph law. If you are driving a vehicle for your employer and it has a potential laden weight that exceeds 3.5 tonnes, you will need a tachograph fitted and be required to use it.

There are a very small number of exemptions and variations to tachograph legislation and EC rules. If you believe that your particular business activity may be exempt from the legislation, ensure that you obtain a judgement in writing to this effect from the Traffic Commissioners (DTLR) in your area. Alternatively visit their official website at http://www.roads.detr.gov.uk for further details.

What is a tachograph?

The word 'tachograph' is commonly used to describe two physical items: the head unit and the paper chart. In this chapter, we will use the term 'tachograph' to refer to that actual head unit, and 'chart' to refer to the paper disc that is inserted in the head unit.

Pictured below is a common tachograph unit.

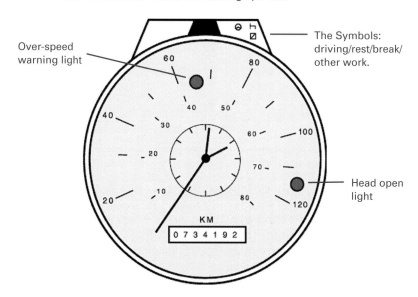

Over-speed warning light

The Symbols: driving/rest/break/ other work.

Head open light

KM
0 7 3 4 1 9 2

The chart

Below is a picture of a tachograph chart. The chart is a standard item which has areas marked on it to record information about speed, distance and driving time.

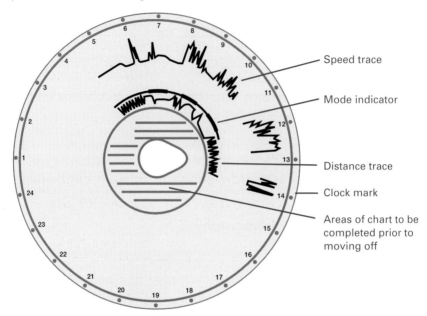

Speed trace

Mode indicator

Distance trace

Clock mark

Areas of chart to be completed prior to moving off

The basic rules of using a tachograph

When you start your day's work, you should complete all the details contained within the centre circle on the front of the chart; name, intended destination and number of kilometres shown on odometer at start of the day. Open the tachograph head unit and insert the chart face down carefully, making sure that the chart is aligned with the pear-shaped spigot. Carefully shut the head unit and lock it, check that the unit is closed properly and make sure the head open warning light is not illuminated. The chart should remain in the unit until the end of your working day.

Remember, at no time during the day are you permitted to open the unit. If you are asked by a police officer or Department of Transport vehicle inspectorate officer to produce the current chart, ensure that the officer signs the chart and notes on it at what time the chart was removed. If charts are seized, ask the officer to sign the replacement chart and make a note as to the number of charts taken, along with a contact telephone number. In most cases you will be issued with a receipt. Make sure you keep this safe and hand it in to your transport manager at your earliest opportunity. Whilst driving, you must have in your possession the charts for your current week's driving along with the last chart for the previous week. Get into the habit of giving all the charts that fall outside this criterion to your transport manager, as it is an offence by the driver to retain charts for more than 21 days. Make sure that you keep all your charts clean and in good condition, failing to do this may lead to prosecution. Make sure that you have sufficient charts to complete your journey. You must always have at least one spare chart in your possession.

Driver's hours

The diagrams below show permitted driving hours and rest periods.

The recognised working week starts on Monday at 00.00 hrs and ends on the following Sunday at 24.00 hrs.

For every 4.5 hours of driving time, you must take a 45-minutes rest break. The rest break can be divided into shorter periods, but rest breaks of less than 15 minutes do not count towards the 45-minutes rest period. Once a 45-minute rest period has been accrued, the driving hours slate is wiped clean, so to speak. Below you can see some acceptable driving patterns.

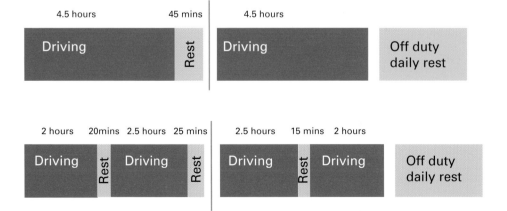

The following example is not acceptable. See if you can work out why that is the case.

2 hours	45 mins	3 hours	30 mins	2 hours	
Driving	Rest	Driving	Rest	Driving	Off duty daily rest

Daily rest

The daily rest period must be a minimum of 11 hours. Alternatively, a 12-hour daily rest period may be taken which may be split into two or three separate periods. This includes at least one period of eight hours without interruption, and the other periods being no less than one hour each. The daily rest period may be reduced to nine hours three times in a week; however, these reduced hours must be paid back (i.e. made up to the original prescribed period) before the end of the following week, and each of these two-hour periods must be appended to an uninterrupted eight-hour rest period.

Weekly rest

A weekly rest period must be taken following no more than six driving days. The weekly rest period is a minimum of 45 hours. This may be reduced to 36 hours if the vehicle is at its normal operating base. If the vehicle is away from the operating base then the weekly rest may, on occasions, be reduced to 24 hours. If either of these reductions is applied, then the shortfall must be repaid as an uninterrupted block before the end of the third week following the day the reduced rest period was taken.

In any fortnight, the driver must not exceed 90 hours of total driving time.

Operating rules

A tachograph head unit must be calibrated on initial installation and then checked every two years. Once the unit is six years old, it should be re-calibrated. The sticker that shows when the last calibration or two-yearly inspection was carried out is located inside the head unit.

Be aware that if you replace tyres on the vehicle at any time, they must be the same size as the tyres fitted when the tachograph was calibrated. The Department of Transport plate, which is attached to the vehicle, will stipulate the correct tyre size and any deviation from this specification will render you liable to prosecution.

Remember to check the tachograph clock. It is important that the tachograph clock reads the correct time. If the vehicle has just returned from the workshop, check the battery wasn't disconnected, causing the clock to be inaccurate. It is also important to make sure the clock is correct in terms of a.m. and p.m.

Whilst working with a vehicle that is fitted with a tachograph, you must remember to switch the device between the driving mode, rest mode and other work mode when appropriate.

Driving – this is the mode that the tachograph should be set to whilst driving.

Other Work – this is the mode that should be selected whilst you are carrying out such duties as loading/unloading.

Rest/Break – select this mode when you take a rest break – remember a rest break must be at least 15 minutes to count.

It is important that you ensure the tachograph is in the correct mode for the activity you are carrying out. If the device is set to the rest mode or other work, all vehicle movements are still recorded on the chart.

Tachographs are highly sensitive devices; any attempt to alter the traces recorded may easily be spotted by a trained examiner. For example, on each occasion the head is opened the chart will be marked and should the recording needle be bent to reduce the maximum speeds recorded, the trace will drop below the base line when the vehicle comes to a rest. Don't ever be tempted to tamper with the head unit or chart. Drivers caught tampering with tachographs will incur large fines and could even face imprisonment.

Tachograph overview

This chapter has covered the basic elements surrounding the use and rules associated with using vehicles fitted with tachographs, and should be viewed as a very basic introduction to tachograph law. The information contained within this chapter is by no means a definitive guide to the subject; its primary aim is to provide a clear and concise first step in understanding this fairly complex issue. If you would like to learn more about tachographs and driver's hours, enrol on a tachograph users course.

To recap, here are a few dos and don'ts to consider when using a tachograph.

The dos

- make sure that you have the correct type of chart for the head unit that is fitted in the vehicle
- make sure that the charts are kept clean and in good condition
- make sure that you complete the centre of the chart prior to inserting the chart
- hand in all charts completed prior to the last day of your previous week's driving
- make sure the calibrations and 2-yearly checks are up to date
- make sure the clock is set to the correct time.

The don'ts

- never drive without a chart inserted in the tachograph
- never open the unit during your driving day
- never be tempted to tamper with the unit in any way
- never leave a chart in the head unit for more than 24 hours
- never switch between modes whilst the vehicle is in motion.

Review

In this chapter we have looked at:

Vehicles which need tachograph units fitted

How to complete a chart for use and insert it correctly

Practical advice for day-to-day use of a tachograph

The law on driver's hours and rest periods

Appendices

Choosing a car for safety

Many company car drivers find themselves in the fortunate position of being able to pick and choose the vehicle they drive. Many drivers will make a selection based on 0 – 60mph times, top speeds, alloy wheels and boot spoilers. The reality is that to get the most out of your vehicle, your selection must be well researched.

First, identify the primary safety features of the vehicle such as ABS brakes, traction control, electronic stability control, high level brake lights and so on, ensuring that the vehicle you choose has as many of these features as possible. The next set of comparisons needs to be based on the secondary safety features – these are the items that prove their value when a vehicle is actually involved in a collision such as airbags, seatbelt pretensioners, side impact beams, head restraints and crumple zones. Below you will find a list of features that you should consider before looking at items such as alloy wheels and metallic paint.

Motor manufacturers are obliged to subject their vehicles to standard crash tests controlled by the New Car Assessment Programme (NCAP). Every new vehicle is given a rating from 1 to 5, the higher the grade awarded the better the vehicle will protect the occupants in a collision.

Use the checklist below to ensure that the vehicle you choose will provide adequate safety and comfort for you and your passengers.

- [ ] at least two airbags – Driver and passenger

- [ ] ABS brakes

- [ ] NCAP 3 or higher

- [ ] side impact beams and side airbags

- [ ] air conditioning

Once you have selected a suitable vehicle, it is important that you know how to obtain the maximum benefit from each of the devices. Below are some points to note about airbags and head restraints.

Airbags

Never sit too close to the steering wheel, always allow sufficient space for the airbag to inflate. A standard airbag when fully inflated will have a diameter of approximately 35cm and a depth of 25cm. You should aim to sit with your chest no closer than 25cm from the wheel centre.

Never place a rear facing child seat in the front seat of a car fitted with a passenger airbag. If you are unsure look for this symbol.

Head restraints

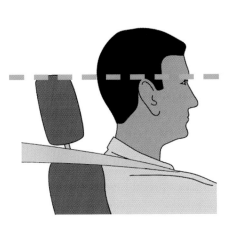

Many drivers fail to recognise the safety benefits of a suitably adjusted head restraint. In the event of a sudden frontal or rear impact, the occupants of a motor vehicle will be thrown forward violently and then backward. The purpose of a head restraint is to stop the head from being forced backward over the seat back, which could lead to serious neck injuries. When adjusting your head restraint ensure that the top edge of it is level or at least in line with the tops of your ears.

When selecting a replacement vehicle you would be well advised to adopt the recommendations found on this page and view these safety features as being the minimum requirements. The right choice of vehicle could prove to be a lifesaver one day!

Roadside first aid

Take some time to read through this section carefully – you never know when someone's life may depend on it!

At the scene of a collision your first priority is to ensure that you are safe and to protect the scene. Position your vehicle safely and use your hazard lights and other methods of communication to highlight to other road users that there is a problem ahead. Carefully assess the collision site without placing yourself in danger from traffic, fire, etc.

The second priority is to alert the emergency services. They will want to know the exact location of the incident, the number of casualties and their general condition. If at all possible, instruct another person to do this whilst you remain with the casualty, and ensure that they will return to confirm that this has been done.

Unless it is absolutely essential, you should avoid moving casualties; do not remove a motorcyclist's crash helmet (unless it is absolutely necessary to do so to protect their airway) and refrain from giving the injured anything to eat or drink. Try and make the injured as comfortable as possible and help them to keep warm. Remain with the casualty until professional help arrives, keep reassuring the injured and encourage them by telling them that help is on its way.

Bleeding. If the casualty is bleeding heavily, use a clean item of clothing to act as a pressure pad. Apply the pad directly to the wound and press hard; if possible elevate a wounded limb to reduce blood flow.

Burns. If a casualty has suffered burns, gently pour cold water over the affected area for as long as 10–20 minutes if possible. Never try and remove any clothing that has stuck to the burn. No cream or lotion should be administered to a burns patient; neither should blisters be burst or loose skin removed. If possible, any rings, belts or watches should be carefully removed as the affected area is likely to swell soon after the injury has been sustained.

Broken bones. If you suspect that the casualty is suffering from a broken bone, there is little to do other than to make the patient as comfortable as possible and to support the injured area using a blanket, rolled up coat or some similar item.

If you need to care for an unconscious casualty, there are three main things you must consider: airway, breathing and circulation. Many first aiders simply refer to this as the **ABC** of first aid.

Airway. It is vital that you ensure that the casualty's airway is clear of any obstruction. Gently tilt the head backwards with a hand on the forehead, check the mouth for any obvious obstructions and lift the chin.

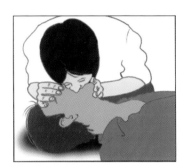

Breathing. Check carefully to see if the casualty is breathing. If you are sure that there is no obstruction to the airway and that the casualty is not breathing then you must commence resuscitation. Pinch the nose and blow into the mouth until you see the chest rise. Give two effective breaths and then look for signs of a circulation.

Circulation. Look for signs of a circulation such as movement, normal colour and normal breathing.

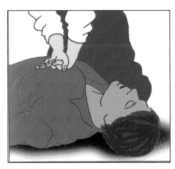

If you are sure that there is no ciruclation present, you may commence chest compressions. Ideally this procedure should be carried out by a qualified first aider. Keep your arms straight and using the heel of your hand apply sufficient pressure in the centre of the chest, along the breast bone, until it lowers by about 4–5cm. Relax your arms at this point and then reapply the same pressure. Carry out 15 chest compressions and then inflate the lungs twice. Chest compressions should be carried out at a rate of 100 per minute.

Call for an ambulance as soon as possible.

If carrying out resuscitation on an infant, be very gentle when inflating the lungs, covering the nose and mouth with your own mouth. Apply very light pressure with two fingers when performing chest compressions, and lower the chest by no more than a third of its depth for children over two years old. Compressions should be at the rate of 100 per minute, and lung inflations at 20 per minute.

If you have never received professional instruction on these or other first aid procedures, you should enrol on a first aid course at your earliest opportunity. This guide should be viewed as an *aide-mémoire* for the trained first aider and should not be considered as an alternative to formal first aid training.

Roadworthiness check

Before you start to drive you should ensure that your vehicle is roadworthy. Carry out the following checks:

- ☐ visual examination of the exterior for damage or defects
- ☐ tools and jack are present and in good order
- ☐ wheels in good order and nuts secure
  (do not over-tighten, especially with alloy wheels)
- ☐ tyres – check all the tyres, including the spare for:
  - damage
  - tread depth
  - pressure (pressure settings are only accurate when tyres are cold)
  - compatibility of type
- ☐ adequate fuel, oil, water, windscreen wash and other fluids
- ☐ fan belt in good condition and correctly tensioned
- ☐ lights – including high intensity foglights, indicators, reversing and brakelights – in working order
- ☐ windscreen wipers and washers in good condition
- ☐ horn working correctly
- ☐ fire extinguisher present and in working order
- ☐ all glass clean – windows inside and out, lenses, mirrors

A useful aid to remember the key points to check is:

P	**O**	**W**	**E**	**R**
petrol	oil	water	electrics	rubber (tyres and wipers)

Pre-driving check

Carry out this check every time you get into a vehicle. Make sure you are familiar with the position and operation of the controls, auxiliary controls and instruments before setting off:

- ☐ handbrake on, gear in neutral

- ☐ identify engine type; type of drive (front-, rear- or four-wheel); type of gearbox (automatic or manual)

- ☐ identify additional driving aids (ABS, traction control, adaptive suspension)

- ☐ adjust seat (position, rake and height, if adjustable) to give good all-round vision and good access to the controls

- ☐ handbrake and footbrake respond firmly

- ☐ number and position of gears, position of reverse gear

- ☐ position of controls and auxiliaries

- ☐ doors are securely closed

Switch on ignition, note warning lights; set manual choke if necessary and start engine. Continue with these checks:

- ☐ after system becomes operational check the instruments; if any of the earlier checks could not be completed before ignition or start up, do them now

- ☐ carry out stationary brake test to ensure the system is working

- ☐ adjust mirrors, inside and out, to give best view

- ☐ make sure all the auxiliaries are working

- ☐ check gauges and warning lights

- ☐ check seat belt – not frayed or twisted, locks when tugged, releases on depressing the button, properly adjusted – and then fit it

- ☐ check in mirrors, select gear, check over shoulder, release handbrake (in automatics keep footbrake depressed before engaging DRIVE), move off when safe

As soon as possible after moving off carry out a moving brake test (see page 80). Check the gauges and warning lights at intervals during the journey, take action if necessary.

Glossary

ABS
See Antilock braking system

Acceleration sense
The ability to vary vehicle speed in response to changing road and traffic conditions by accurate use of the accelerator. *See page 73*

Antilock braking system
A braking system which retains the ability to steer during harsh or emergency braking. Also known as ABS. *See page 32, 93*

Aquaplaning
A serious loss of steering and braking control caused by a wedge of water building up between the front tyres and the road surface. *See page 34*

Auxiliaries
The auxiliary controls on a vehicle as distinct from the major controls. Examples of the auxiliaries are: horn, indicators, lights, wipers, washers, heater and ventilation controls. *See Controls, Instruments*

Blind spots
Areas around a vehicle which the driver cannot see because the bodywork blocks sight or the mirrors do not cover these areas. *See page 62.*

Bottom gear
See Gears

Cadence or rhythm braking
A method of braking in slippery conditions which uses repeated application of the brakes to obtain some steering control while braking. The brakes are sharply applied, to momentarily hold the wheels locked, and then released again to regain steering. This sequence is repeated deliberately until sufficient road speed is lost. Braking occurs while the brakes are on, steering while they are off. *See pages 85, 99*

Camber
The convex slope across a road surface designed to assist drainage. Camber falls from the crown of the road to the edges. It has an effect on cornering which differs according to whether the bend is to the right or the left. *See page 117*

Central differential
The differential in a four-wheel drive vehicle which allows the front and rear wheels to revolve at different speeds.

Controls
The major controls of a vehicle are the accelerator, brakes, clutch, gear-stick, steering wheel. *See Auxiliaries, Instruments*

Cornering
Cornering is used to mean driving a car round a corner, curve or bend. Its meaning is not restricted to corners. *See page 114*

Cylinder compression
See Engine compression

Engine compression
The compression of gases in the cylinders of an internal combustion engine. Compression uses energy so, when deceleration reduces the fuel supply to the engine, energy for compression is taken from the road wheels, thereby slowing them down.

Following position
The distance at which it is safe to follow a vehicle in front. This distance varies according to the circumstances. *See pages 130, 131*

Gears

The mechanism which converts the engine output into different speed and power combinations at the road wheels. A high gear is a gear which drives the road wheels faster; a low gear is a gear which drives the road wheels more slowly. Top gear is the highest gear; bottom gear is the lowest gear. In most cars top gear is gear 4 or 5; bottom gear is gear 1.

Hazard/hazardous

Any thing or situation that has the potential for danger. *See page 46*

High gear

See Gears

Information phase

First phase of the system of vehicle control which underlies the other phases. *See page 47, 49*

Instruments

The gauges, dials, warning lights, etc. of a vehicle that give information about how it is functioning: for example, the speedometer, oil warning light and main beam indicator. *See Auxiliaries, Controls*

Limit point

The limit point is the furthest point along a road to which you have an uninterrupted view of the road surface. On a level stretch of road this will be where the right-hand side of the road appears to intersect with the left-hand side of the road. The limit point is used in a system of cornering called limit point analysis. *See page 118*

Low gear

See Gears

Nearside

The left side of a vehicle or animal looking forward from the driver's position. *See also Offside*

Offside

The right side of a vehicle or animal looking forward from the driver's position. *See also Nearside*

Oversteer

The tendency of a vehicle to turn more than you would expect for the amount of turn given to the steering wheel. Contrast with understeer. *See page 116*

Overtaking position

The position adopted behind another vehicle in readiness to overtake when a safe opportunity arises. It is closer than the following position and reduces the time you have to react to actions of the vehicle in front. It should only be adopted if you know there are no hazards ahead which might cause the vehicle in front to brake suddenly. *See page 132*

POWER check

An aid for remembering the key items to check before starting a journey: Petrol, Oil, Water, Electrics, Rubber (tyres and wipers). *See page 178*

Pull–push steering

A steering technique. *See page 88*

Revs

The number of engine revolutions per minute.

Rhythm braking

See Cadence braking

Road users

Any user of the highway: vehicles, cyclists, pedestrians, animals. The term is used to emphasise the need to be aware of everything on the highway, not just vehicles.

Roadside marker posts

Posts marking the edge of the road, displaying red reflective studs on the nearside of the road and white reflective studs on the offside of the road.

Rotational steering
A steering technique. *See page 89*

Safe stopping distance rule
This rule is one of the basic safety considerations when driving. It controls your speed by relating speed to the ability to stop. Always drive so that you are able to stop on your own side of the road in the distance you can see to be clear. *See page 81*

Scanning
Method of observation. The use of regular visual sweeps of the whole of the driving environment – the distance, the mid-ground, the foreground, sides and rear – to ensure that the driver is aware of everything that is happening.
See pages 22, 59

Superelevation
Superelevation is the banking up of a section of road towards the outside edge of the curve. This makes the slope favourable for cornering in both directions. *See page 117*

The system – the system of vehicle control
A systematic way of approaching and negotiating hazards that emphasises safety and is central to *Fleetcraft*. It is fully explained in Chapter 6.

Top gear
See Gears

Traction
The grip of a tyre on the road surface.

Traction control systems
Traction control improves vehicle stability and assists steering by controlling excess wheel slip on individual wheels and reducing engine power to maintain tyre grip. *See page 94*

Understeer
The tendency of a vehicle to turn less than you expect for the amount of turn you give to the steering wheel. Contrast with oversteer.
See page 116

Undertaking
Overtaking on the nearside in situations which contravene the *Highway Code*.

Wheel slip
The difference between the velocity of the vehicle and the velocity of the outer circumference of the tyre, usually expressed as a percentage.

Index